G · BRAQUE

PHAIDON

G·BRAQUE

BY JOHN RUSSELL

WITH EIGHTY ILLUSTRATIONS
INCLUDING TWENTY-FOUR IN COLOUR
SELECTED BY RENÉ BEN SUSSAN

THE PHAIDON PRESS·LONDON

TO

DORA MAAR

THE PAINTINGS OF GEORGES BRAQUE ARE REPRODUCED
BY ARRANGEMENT WITH ASSOCIATION POUR LA DIFFUSION
DES ARTS GRAPHIQUES ET PLASTIQUES · PARIS

ALL RIGHTS RESERVED
BY PHAIDON PRESS LTD · LONDON

MADE IN GREAT BRITAIN 1959
TEXT PRINTED BY GEO · GIBBONS LTD · LEICESTER
PLATES PRINTED BY HENRY STONE & SON LTD · BANBURY

INTRODUCTION

I N ART, in music, in literature, in science and in the exploration of human nature, the period immediately preceding the war of 1914-18 was one of the most brilliant of which we have record. There is, in a real sense, literature before Proust, and literature after him; painting before, and painting after, cubism; music before, and music after, the development of the twelve-note system; physics before, and physics after, Einstein and Rutherford; and, where our knowledge of human beings is concerned, psychoanalysis and the scientific study of primitive societies have likewise produced, even among those who still resist them, a complete break with the past.

In considering all this, it is difficult to pick on any one particular year as the hinge on which modern life, as we know it, swung into view. But perhaps 1908 has the strongest claim. Proust's novel-series was, as yet, foreshadowed only in letters to one or two friends; but both Berg and Webern produced their op. 1 in 1908, and in Schönberg's op. 11 and 15 the traditional tonal system was, for the first time, entirely suspended. Rutherford was awarded the Nobel Prize. At a one-day meeting in Salzburg there was held the first international Psychoanalytical Congress; for the first and last time Freud, Jung, Adler, Stekel, Trotter and Ernest Jones met together in conference and talked over what Lionel Trilling was later to call 'the only systematic account of the human mind which, in point of subtlety and complexity, of interest and tragic power, deserves to stand beside the chaotic mass of psychological insights which literature has accumulated throughout the centuries'. For the emergence of anthropology as *the* humane science of the twentieth century—the science of society, in fact, and the one which may still teach us how to live with one another—it is yet more difficult to assign a specific date; but in 1908 Frazer was preparing his enlarged *Golden Bough*, Malinowski took his doctor's degree at Cracow, and Claude Lévi-Strauss was born.

The evolution of cubism was not, of course, the only phenomenon of interest or importance, where painting was concerned, in the period under review. But in so far as it involved the rejection of much that had been taken for granted since the Renaissance, it could claim to be the most radical, the most searching, and the most audacious of developments. And here there can, for once, be no doubt of the decisive date; for it was in November, 1908, that Daniel-Henry Kahnweiler put on the first and only one-man show to be held at his gallery at No. 28 rue Vignon, just behind the Madeleine. Braque was the painter thus honoured, there were twenty-seven pictures on the walls, the catalogue was prefaced by Apollinaire, and it was in relation to this exhibition that the word 'cubism' was first used.

Rare is the exhibition that has not a drama behind it, even if some variant of incapacity is all too often that drama's main subject. In Braque's case, the elements of conflict were two-fold. The one-man show, as such, was still something of a novelty, and Braque, at the outset of his career, had done well in the large mixed exhibitions which were still, as they had been in Delacroix's day, the natural outlet for a debutant. At the Salon des Indépendants in March, 1907, he had sold all six of his pictures, at prices from 75 to 200 francs; but when he submitted seven new canvases to the Salon d'Automne in the following year they were turned down. Marquet and Charles Guérin were ready to 'vote in' two of the rejected canvases, but Braque preferred to show his new pictures in bulk, and on their own; and Kahnweiler, who since the autumn of 1907 had had the exclusivity of Braque's work, must also have felt that the moment was crucial for the development of the twenty-six-year old painter.

And of course it is easy enough for us today to recognise that this was, in effect, one of the most important exhibitions of the twentieth century. But to those who had ventured a pound or two on the landscapes which Braque had painted at Antwerp in 1906, or in the south of France in the winter of 1906-07, it may well have seemed perverse and disconcerting. Vauxcelles may, in fact, have been voicing a general opinion when he complained, in his famous article in *Gil Blas*, that Braque 'mistreats form and reduces everything—sites, figures, houses—to geometric outlines, to *cubes*'.

Disappointment may, moreover, have been all the greater because Braque had, even in his relatively clumsy beginnings, a quality of ingratiation which had been quick to find its mark. It can be an enormous help to an artist to have painting 'in the air' around him; and Braque, in this respect, was as well favoured as anyone since Tintoretto. At Argenteuil, where he was born at No. 40 rue de l'Hôtel Dieu on May 13th, 1882, Manet, Monet and Renoir had spent part of the summer together in 1874; and when Braque was a very small boy a new house was pointed out to him as the property of Monsieur Caillebotte, the patron of the Impressionists. In 1890 or thereabouts, when the family moved to Le Havre, Boudin and Corot were almost palpably present, not merely in the pictures of theirs which were to be found in the local museum, but in the splendour and nobility of the scenes which they had been the first to set down as they deserved. And among his acquaintances was Raoul Dufy, five years his senior, whose brother taught Braque the flute.

These auguries were complemented by a family atmosphere which must have been almost ideally favourable to the development of a gift such as Braque's. Painting of one sort or another was what kept the Braque family going; Braque's father and grandfather were house-painters by profession and Sunday painters by choice. Everything was done that could be done to help Braque forward; and his apprenticeship to the family profession was much more than a form of insurance against failure. He drew from it, in the first place, the regard for fine craftsmanship which has been remarked a thousand times by commentators on his work; next, a repertory of textures vastly subtler and more various than those normally available to a *beaux-arts* student in his final year; and along with these, habits of patience and perseverance which were exactly suited to his gifts. '*Heureusement, j'avais l'esprit lent,*' he still says of his beginnings; and his was, in effect, a solitary, slow-moving nature. When his mind was made up, however, he was correspondingly massive and powerful in his attack upon the matter in hand. Much can be learnt, in this connection, from Henri-Pierre Roché's story of how Braque, as an amateur boxer, had an impenetrable 'défense anglaise' and could so wear down the bigger and wilder Derain that eventually he would weaken and be at the mercy of a single well-judged blow from Braque.

Braque was a conscientious student. But he followed the classic modern-art pattern in learning less from formal 'art education' than from his friends, and from those major exhibitions which are one of the twentieth century's chief contributions to the architecture of a painting career. To be the friend of Dufy and Othon Friesz, in Le Havre, and of Picabia and Marie Laurencin in Paris, was to be assured of knowing, or at any rate of hearing, what was going forward, even if nothing very personal seemed to emerge from Braque's years of study at the Académie Humbert and elsewhere. When he 'left school' for good in 1904 and set up on his own in Montmartre nobody took him for an artist of genius; so secretive was his nature that an art-dealer who did a year's military service with him in 1901-02 had no idea that he had ever done any painting. A singer, yes; or a virtuoso of the dance-floor; or a gifted accordeonist; but a painter? His fellow-conscripts would have been greatly amazed.

Braque's individuality would seem to have been liberated at one stroke by the experience of seeing, at the Salon d'Automne of 1905, the room devoted to the *fauves*. His excitement lasted a bare two years ('You can't live your whole life in a state of paroxysm', as he said later) and today he inclines to mark down even the best productions of the *fauves*. But at the time their effect was very great; and if, indeed, there were such a thing as an aesthetic of pure exhilaration, nothing could more vividly contribute to it than the best of the pictures painted at Collioure by Matisse and Derain in 1905. 'Matisse and Derain opened the road for me,' is one of Braque's most oft-quoted remarks; but on the technical side some credit should go to Friesz, lower-spirited by nature than either Matisse or Derain, who was Braque's companion in Antwerp in the summer of 1906. Braque took a characteristically long time to integrate into his instinctively cautious and tentative style of painting the colossal energy and plain bright statements which were the mark of the *fauves;* and indeed he never contrived, and perhaps never aimed, to do so completely. In a painting like *The Mast, Antwerp,* 1906 (Plate 1), there lingers an element of objective weather-reporting, and even in the pictures done at L'Estaque in the autumn and winter of 1906–07 the eye is often encouraged to negotiate its way from tone to tone, as against the abrupt leaps and salutary oppositions of authentic *fauve* practice. Many pictures of this period are awkward in construction, with the foreground buckled into place by a balustrade or fence of some kind; and whereas Matisse or Derain would proceed in a torrent of rectangular strokes, each the size of a domino, Braque would often duck back to a flowing, not to say serpentine line (4). Nor was the gamut of colour in which the *fauves* excelled quite suited to his more deliberate methods; where Vlaminck, for instance, tried to scale the topmost heights of excitement with scarlet and high yellow Braque turned rather to sun-blanched pink and that refinement of violet which was the ancient Chinese colour for mourning.

The purely physical stimulus of the *fauve* aesthetic did not sustain Braque for long. Nor did the South, in itself, maintain its interest. As Braque once said to Jean Paulhan: 'The first year (1906–07) there was the pure enthusiasm, the astonishment of the Parisian who discovers the Midi. The next year, that had already changed. I should have had to push on down to Senegal to get the same result. You can't count on enthusiasm for more than ten months.' Braque's basic ambitions were, in any case, of a different kind from those of the *Fauves.* Classical perspective was not his strongest point, and in designing his pictures he often had to plug up the foreground with a massive, easily-deciphered horizontal or diagonal, and from there work backwards towards the horizon. Alternatively he would touch in the sky at the top of the picture and bring the composition tumbling down-hill until it seemed likely to finish up in the observer's lap. Where the scene offered horizontals of its own making (as in the harbours of Antwerp and La Ciotat) Braque would rely on them to strengthen the design; when Nature tended, on the other hand, to the serpentine line of a wooded hill backed up against the sky, Braque came nearer to an unbroken arabesque, an almost decorative use of line, than to the chubby strokes with which Derain, for one, would probably have attacked the same scene.

For weaknesses of this sort there was compensation in the charm and delicacy of Braque's colour, which remained individual even when, for a time, he tried his hand at a variant of the pointillism employed by Signac and Cross at St. Tropez and elsewhere. But by the autumn of 1907 one of the master-principles of Braque's work was beginning to make itself felt.

He has himself referred to this more than once in his notebooks—saying for instance that 'Progress in art consists not in extending one's limits, but in knowing them better', and that 'Limited means bring new forms into being, shape style, and prompt the artist to create'. And, again, 'All "effects", in art, do violence to the truth.'

Braque noted down these thoughts towards the end of the war of 1914-18—at a time, that is to say, when he had already left his mark upon the history of art. But they are also illuminating, I think, when applied to those earlier paintings in which the true nature of his genius is not yet revealed. For it was *because* Braque was not a 'brilliant student' and could not have carried off the effects of virtuosity with which many young painters burst upon the world that he was able to look steadily round at what was going on in art and, eventually, to happen on the two artists who were to mean most to him, Cézanne and Picasso. Cubism came into being in response to the analysis of certain specific limitations in Braque's equipment; able to proceed only to a limited degree with the 'traditional' re-constitution of Nature for pictorial ends, he went in search of new centres of resistance. 'We could not, in any case,' he said to Georges Duthuit, 'have progressed further with the methods in use at that time. All those who, since then, have achieved something have sought out resistances.'

To re-trace exactly the steps by which Braque arrived not merely at a new 'style', but at a new *kind* of painting is not easy. For one thing, Braque's progressive detachment from the Impressionist legacy—the single viewpoint, the exact registration of light, the reliance upon a given motif— was accomplished in reply to promptings for which even he himself has always found it difficult to find a name. 'At such a time,' he said in 1954, 'one has to follow dictates which are almost unconscious, because there is no knowing what will happen. The adventure through which one is living is one in which consciousness plays no part.' The other obstacle to elucidation is the fact that cubism was the joint creation of Braque and Picasso, and that nobody, least of all the two painters themselves, has ever managed—or, in their case, perhaps wished—to establish the relative importance of their roles.

As far as Cézanne is concerned, on the other hand, the influence is clearly finger-posted—as much in the sudden simplification and angularity of the forms as in the progressive narrowing-down of the palette to pale ochre and wild-asparagus green. But Braque was drawn to Cézanne by an attraction that went far beyond affinity of style: 'everything about him was sympathetic to me, the man, his character, everything. . . .'. And, again from his notebooks, a remark that tells us much: 'some pictures make one think of the artist, others of the man. I have often heard people speak of Manet's talent, but never anyone of Cézanne's.'

9

Braque's beginnings as a painter of world-class date from 1907, the year of the Cézanne exhibitions at the Salon d'Automne and Bernheim-Jeune, and of his meetings with Apollinaire and Picasso, and of his contract with Kahnweiler. Like many French poets and men of letters, Apollinaire was deeply interested in art and did all that he could to champion the artists he admired. More recently both artists and art-historians have tended to blow upon the authenticity and originality of Apollinaire's perceptions, and Braque himself has said roundly that he 'could not tell a Raphael from a Rubens'. In all this there seems an element of ingratitude, in some cases, and envy, in others; for, whether or not Apollinaire took the words out of his painter-friends' mouths, the fact remains that he, a man of genius in his own right, came out in favour of the best new artists of the day at a time when those artists could count their henchmen in twos and threes.

It was through Apollinaire, in any case, and indirectly through Kahn-weiler that Braque and Picasso met in the autumn of 1907. One of the first results of this was that Braque went to Picasso's studio in Montmartre and there saw the *Demoiselles d'Avignon*, which Picasso had completed in the spring of the same year. Braque was characteristically slow to accept the implications of what Mr. Douglas Cooper has succinctly described as 'a revolutionary and experimental picture executed in a conceptual, not a perceptual, idiom and in which Pompeian, Iberian and Negro influences were uncomfortably blended'. But that he was deeply stirred is evident as much in the violence of his first reaction as in the long and painful process of readjustment to which he subjected himself in the winter of 1907-08. The results are to be found both in the monumental *Grand Nu* in the Cuttoli collection and in the drawing of a female nude, which was the inspiration in 1908 of Braque's earliest etching. Braque's idiosyncratic and pinkish tonality persisted, even in the *Grand Nu*, but in other respects he was discarding, one by one, the notions of his first youth. 'It all came of its own accord,' as he once said. 'One day I noticed that I could go on working at my *motif* no matter what the weather might be. I no longer needed the sun, for I took my light everywhere with me.' Next he began (with great difficulty, at first) to work from memory. When he left Paris to spend the summer of 1908 at L'Estaque it soon appeared that Nature was no longer to call the tune. The single viewpoint, on which classical perspective is based, no longer sufficed. It was part of an activity which could now be rejected: that of imitating, more or less fallibly, 'what the eye sees' at a given moment. The new duty of the painter lay elsewhere: in the creation of pictures which were at once self-sufficient works of art and encyclopaedias of information about the objects under examination. Picasso's remark that 'in cubism you paint not what you see, but what you know is there' is still a valid short summary of the subject.

In the landscapes executed in the summer of 1908 (6, 7) the effect of all this was at once apparent. All circumstantial detail vanished: what remained was the minimum that, architecturally speaking, would hold the scene together. Colour was no longer used to describe the trees or buildings in question, but served rather to *build* the picture. Colour had, in fact, abdicated its conventional, purely local connotations and become a constituent part of *le fait pictural*. For anyone with as keen and as personal a sense of colour as Braque, the sacrifice of the private gamut, if one may so call it, is one of the risks which had to be taken but might so easily have led to failure. There was no longer any attempt to make a 'likeness' of the scene which was its pretext; the picturesque elements of the South of France, the bronze earth and the vibrating blue of the sky, have no place in the L'Estaque landscapes of 1908. All that remained of Braque's earlier practice was just occasionally (6, 7) the great sideway-swinging line of a tree that set the *tempo primo* of the composition. Elsewhere all was different; volumes in space are the pictures' main subject, the sky plays no part, the forms are faceted and turn towards the observer at a variety of acute angles. What Carl Einstein, Braque's first monographer, called 'that Platonic monster, the immutable, unchanging spectator' was at last swept aside, and with him went (Einstein again) 'the unity of perspectivist illusion'. All this was, of course, to be borne out more vividly in the analytical cubist pictures of 1911 and later; but already Braque was in revolt against 'scientific perspective, which does not allow one to take full possession of things'. The picture-space had ceased to be a *foire aux illusions*. As Einstein wrote, in 1931, Braque had in hand nothing less than 'une modification radicale, une nouvelle formation des faits, de la vision, et de l'espace'.

Such were the pictures which were rejected by the jury of the Salon d'Automne in 1908. If they were related to Cézanne, it was above all to the classic landscapes painted at Gardanne in 1885-86; the forms of the houses in the *Houses at L'Estaque* might have been quarried from Cézanne's favourite in later life, the *carrières de Bibemus*. And when Braque turned, likewise in the summer of 1908, to still-life painting, Cézanne was again the source of his style. Apollinaire quite rightly said of the pictures of this period that they had 'created a new personal alphabet, of which each letter enjoys universal acceptance'; and this remained true of the *Port in Normandy* (8), done from imagination, and the eight landscapes painted at La Roche-Guyon (9) in the summer of 1909. If we remember the hesitant character of Braque's earlier paintings there is something really astonishing in the cogency and "attack" with which Braque set out his new vision of space. Not that Cézanne was now excluded; in the *Port*, as in the *Viaduct at L'Estaque* of 1908 and the *Donjon at La Roche-Guyon* of 1909, the composition derives from the central pyramid which Cézanne had used in the *Grandes Baigneuses*, now in the

Philadelphia Museum. But in the autumn of 1909, when Braque and Picasso drew close to one another, the period of analytical cubism began, and before long even those who had Apollinaire's alphabet in mind were hard put to spell out the meaning of all that was going on.

Braque has never been interested to impose himself upon the world as a 'personality', with all that the word implies in the way of the cretin's criteria of quality, and he rarely speaks directly of the hazards involved in a career such as his. But I fancy that he would say, with Gide, that 'the world will be saved by one or two people': and once, in talking to Dora Vallier, he likened the beginnings of cubism to Columbus' first voyage across the Atlantic. 'The first time Columbus had only faith and prayer to guide him, and he found the New World. After that, a compass did the work. But real discoveries are made beyond the limits of knowledge.'

For a long time it was believed in this country that Braque stood to Picasso in rather the same relation as Souverbie stands to Braque. But the truth is elsewhere. Certainly Picasso was influenced by the Cézanne exhibitions of 1907 to try his hand, in 1908, at such Cézannesque subjects as *Le Cronstadt*, in which Braque's hat figures, and the series of landscapes painted at La-Rue-des-Bois. But he did not 'catch on' to what Braque was after until a year later, when he spent the summer at Horta de Ebro. There is no question, here, as to who led the way. But there is also no question that, both between 1909 and 1914 and intermittently for many years later, Braque did value Picasso very highly indeed for just the qualities which were lacking in himself; mercurial powers of adaptation, for instance, a demonic virtuosity, and the knack of playing upon the spectator's nerves.

The problem before the two painters was this: how best to paint pictures which were autonomous objects, acknowledging no laws but their own, and yet presenting the observer with the truth about objects in space. Braque proceeded, as always, with a view to minimising the shortcomings of his equipment: 'my cubism,' he said lately, 'was a means I created for my own use, whose primary aim was to put painting within the reach of my own gifts.' In doing this he subjected objects in space to a dose of reality many times stronger, if I may so put it, than that which we normally employ: 'there is a temperature,' he said to Paulhan, 'at which iron becomes malleable and loses the sense of itself. That is the kind of temperature I search for. A picture is made up of disaffected objects.'

In 1954 Braque claimed that he had never wittingly planned to become a painter, and could not remember ever, in all his life, willing himself to do anything at all. 'As Nietzsche said, "An aim is slavery".' His 'aim', in so far as he ever formulated one, was rather to complete himself. 'What I did in the process ended by looking like a picture. And when I sold all six of my paintings at the Indépendants in 1907 I said to myself, "If I wanted to, I could do nothing but paint for the rest of my life".'

All this reads like English understatement when we compare it with the recollections of Braque's contemporaries, who speak on the contrary of his 'inner security' and 'elemental perseverance'. Perhaps the truth is that Braque has known, as well as any painter in history, just how to ride with his gifts. Even he admits, however, that the period from 1909 to 1914 was one of intense exaltation. 'The things that Picasso and I said to one another during those years will never be said again. Nobody could say them, and even if they were said nobody could understand them . . . they would be incomprehensible. But what joy we had from them! All that will end with us. It was rather as if we were two climbers, roped together. . . .'

Something of this exaltation got through to one or two sensitive outsiders—to Pierre Reverdy, the poet, for instance. In his book *Une Aventure Méthodique*, which appeared in 1949 and is ornamented with twenty-eight original lithographs by Braque, Reverdy describes the year 1911, 'when the future was quite bare and the present unusually complex and precarious'. 'I remember,' he goes on, 'the heroic and unsparing discussions, and the pictures, grey, congested, ferociously hermetic, in which the two brave, powerful and almost wholly unknown young men would slake their enormous appetite for reality.' Reverdy goes on to pity those who were there at the time and took no part in the struggle. 'I doubt if ever before in the history of art was there so much sunshine, so many blue skies, so much responsibility so bravely assumed, or so great a gap set between disaster and the hoped-for. . . .'

Before taking leave of landscape, Braque sometimes allowed the intensity of his feelings to take an almost expressionist form—in the *Viaduct at L'Estaque* of 1908, for instance, or in the *Fishing Boats* of 1909, where the planes leap about like porpoises, and in the El Greco-like drama of the *Town on a Hill* of 1909. But when the phase of analytical cubism began in the autumn of 1909, Braque's work began to tend towards the serene and inevitable quality which has been the mark, ever since, of his major paintings. For an impression of his state of mind at that time we shall do better to look at Picasso's *Portrait of Braque* of 1909 than at any of Braque's own paintings; for the portrait has about it an air of sombre violence and obsessional concentration well suited to the great leap forward which Braque was taking at the time.

In the analytical cubist pictures executed in the winter of 1909-10, Braque had two main subjects: still-life, often with musical instruments, and very large figure-paintings, in which the figure is as a rule seated and often carries a stringed instrument of one sort or another. Mr. John Richardson has suggested that the exhibition of Corot's figure-paintings, held in Paris in

13

1909, was probably responsible for the cubists' preoccupation with seated figures; and there is support for this view in the fact that Braque has pinned up in his Paris studio a large coloured reproduction of Corot's noble portrait of Christine Nilsson, in which the sitter carries an instrument of the sort favoured by Braque. Braque has kept in his own collection one of the earliest of his still-lives with musical instruments: dated 1909, it assembles a clarinet, a mandoline, an open score, and the six-sided concertina with which Braque entertained his friends, so Monsieur Roché tells us, with 'music ranging from Bach to the circus'. This picture is immediately legible, even by Victorian standards, although the picture-space seems no deeper than a cigar-box and the top of the table is tilted steeply downwards in accordance with Braque's vision of space as 'tactile'—forming an element, that is to say, in which objects are within reach of the spectator. But within a few months, in the winter of 1909-10, Braque was at work on the tall thin canvases (10, 11) which are among the great paintings of this century; and in these the procedures ('theories' is not the right word) of analytical cubism are seen in maturity. The objects are both seen and lit from several points of view simultaneously; familiar in themselves (and particularly acceptable to Braque because musical instruments literally 'come alive' at our touch) they take on an unfamiliar majesty by the exclusion from the picture of everything in our everyday experience of them which is fugitive, accidental, or contingent. Traditional perspective and illusionist 'space' are abolished. Colour is used constructively, and with no descriptive intent, the dominant tonality often being that of grass burnt brown by the sun. The faceting is more or less continuous, with here and there a naturalistic detail touched in to create an equation or point of suggestive contact between the reality of the picture and the reality of everyday vision. In the *Piano and Mandola*, for instance, where the piano is clearly an upright one, the half-burnt candle in its protruding stick is just such a detail; and there is even a hint, in the long spread of the keyboard at the bottom of the picture, of one of those broad diagonals with which Braque had liked to pull his compositions into place three or four years earlier. In the Basle *Jug and Violin* (11), where the form of the jug is defined with all the masculine vigour and attack which characterised Braque at this period, and the scrolled head of the violin has likewise an emblematic, almost heraldic definition, there occurs at the top of the canvas the *trompe-l'oeil* nail, of which much was made at the time. To introduce so conventional a device into the cascading facets of analytical cubism was interpreted by some as a raid into enemy territory, by others as a concise demonstration of the contrast between the new and the old methods of evoking reality. It seems to me that, over and above its obvious polemical interest, it may relate to a metaphor with which Braque has long been preoccupied, and one that comes out even in pictures painted

14

forty years later; in *The Billiard Table*, for instance, of 1944-52, where a *trompe-l'oeil* coat-hanger intrudes upon the immensely elaborate and delicately articulated scene. 'We can't always,' he wrote in one of his notebooks, 'have our hats in our hands. That's why the hat-stand was invented. And I turned to painting in order to have a peg to hang my ideas on.'

When Braque turned to figure-subjects there were still, at first, a number of explicit allusions to everyday vision. In the *Half-length of a Young Girl* (12), which dates from the summer of 1910, the flower in the hair, the loose-flowing tresses, and the pendant with its cross are all 'laid into' the picture as reality-conductors, although even the head itself, the face, the shoulders and the heavy rolled collar are treated in pure analytical-cubist style. By the spring of 1911, on the other hand, when Braque painted *The Portuguese* (13), cubism was entering what is often called its hermetic phase: legible details were becoming fewer and fewer, and although this picture does, in point of fact, contain much more illustrative matter than is usual in the figure-pictures of the period, there is a great difference between the modelling and the treatment of volumes in *The Portuguese* and the handling of these same problems in the *Jug and Violin* or the *Piano and Mandola*.

Picasso and Braque spent the summer of 1911 at Céret in the Pyrenees; and as Picasso was in particularly trenchant and fertile mood the two painters progressed rapidly to a point at which they might well have vanished over the frontiers of incomprehensibility had they not remained concerned above all with reality. Colour remained severe and sober; not to distract was its first duty. Forms were broken down into flat surfaces, some opaque, others transparent or refractive. Objects, or parts of objects, were no longer isolated, from time to time, but kept firmly subject to the arrowy, sharp-angled movement of the lines which darted to and fro across the picture-surface, now making a shorthand note of the picture's furnishings, now concerned only with its all-over structure and scheme, now defining the interval between one form and the next. Once again Reverdy has something of value to say about this phase of cubism, and about the two painters' attempt to render Matter less opaque, less obstinately shut within itself. The dangers seemed, at the time, extreme: and yet 'nowadays anyone can see that what ensured the salvation of these painters was their immediate and untameable grasp of all that is strongest and humblest in Reality. Instinct and intelligence had told them to hold fast to that; and the touchable meant as much to them as the conceptual.'

Already in *The Portuguese* there are signs of that preoccupation with the 'touchable' which was to steer Braque safely clear of complete impenetrability. I refer, of course, to the stencilled letters and figures which here make one of their first appearances in his work. Henceforward Braque's skills as a painter-decorator were to play a considerable role in the development of

15

cubism, and even in the paintings of the last ten or fifteen years there are renewed instances of their use. For instance, in the *Sunflowers* of 1946, now owned by the Reader's Digest, he has painted both in and out of the ostensible picture a handsome frame of modish design. On another occasion he teased the eventual owner of the picture by incorporating at the foot of his composition a long flat appendix on which is painted a name-plate, 'G. Braque', in elegant and workmanlike style. One could advance many explanations of Braque's motives for darting back and forth in this way from one sort of reality to another, just as Kahnweiler went to Kant and Locke when he wanted to show why analytical cubism put certain things in and left others out. But as far as the initial introduction of stencilled letters is concerned, Braque has himself said that his object was, as always, 'to get as close as I could to reality. . . . These were forms which could not be distorted in any way. The letters, being themselves flat, were not in space; therefore, by contrast, their presence in the picture made it possible to distinguish between those objects which were situated in space and those which were not.' The letters were both a source of narrative detail, like the newspaper in Wilkie's *Reading the Gazette of the Battle of Waterloo*, and a new and subtle instrument of articulation.

The possible uses of Braque's professional skills became a subject of ever greater concern to him when it was clear that cubism had gone about as far as it could usefully go in the way of chastening the picture-substance. The handling of paint in Braque's later masterpieces proves him to be one of the subtlest and most resourceful voluptuaries in the history of art; the more remarkable, therefore, is the self-denial to which he must have sworn himself in the late summer and autumn of 1911. He was as loyal as anyone could be to the field-grey uniform of the day, even if a stroke or two of dark red or azure are sometimes allowed to lighten the complex design.

The Musée d'Art Moderne's so-called *Guéridon* of 1911(14) is a painting which, though retrogressive in style in so far as it harks back to the analytical paintings of the previous year, none the less introduces for the first time one of Braque's most favourite subjects: the still-life in which a robust and heavily-laden table is tipped well forward towards the spectator and the bottom of the canvas is filled out with its sturdy legs. It has none of the congestion of the hermetic ovals, *Still Life with Dice*, *Pipe and Glasses* and *Soda* which also date from 1911; its general tone is, on the contrary, both monumental and relaxed, with the great unbroken curve of the table-edge to echo the faceted belly of the instrument and a restricted number of planes to float like the flaps of open envelopes among the isolated crotchets, the rolled music-paper and the violin-head which combine to suggest that in this picture Braque is in some sense reverting to the things he loves best. (This picture was formerly, and more accurately, entitled *The Round Table*.)

Music and its attributes played a great part in the subject-matter of Braque's paintings between 1912 and the outbreak of war in August, 1914. But in handling the familiar forms of violin, guitar, flageolet, harp, and sheet-music, and in conjuring before us such relevant words as BACH, BAL and VALSE, Braque did not by any means remain set in his earlier ways. On the contrary; the two years before the war were unprecedentedly rich in technical invention. Much of this invention flowed logically from the introduction of flat forms (stencilled letters initially) into the pictures painted in 1911. But the letters were not important merely for their flatness: there was also the consideration that they were visitor-objects, intruders from the world of everyday fact. This gave them a double importance for painters whose aim was to produce pictures which would co-exist with nature on terms of equality. In the struggle to achieve this, the traditional blandishments of the illusionist-painter had been discarded, one by one; the hermetic-cubist pictures which eventually resulted contrived, none the less, to give a full and profound experience both of space and of the sensuous and tactile reality of objects. Colour, was, however, the great casualty of these procedures; and so, when Picasso and Braque settled down to work at Sorgues, near Avignon, in July 1912, their main object was to find a valid way of re-introducing into their pictures an element of constructive colour. That colour and form should be dissociated was axiomatic, and must somehow be demonstrated.

At the same time both painters were anxious, I think, to arrive at a less penitential variety of picture-substance without relapsing into the trumpery attractions, as they saw them, of *la belle peinture*. Neither Braque nor Picasso was of a nature to keep for long to the total sobriety of *matière* which is characteristic of hermetic cubism. And as Braque has always had an almost religious regard for the original substances from which the world is made up—he delights, for instance, in the French word *limon*, which figures so bravely in the Book of Genesis—he began at this time to mix alien matter into his pigments: ashes from his stove, sand, wood-shavings, metal-filings, tobacco. But the notion that colour *is* texture did not solve the immediate problem, though it gave Braque a new instrument, and one which he has used to marvellous effect in more recent times. Something other than the cross-breeding of paint was clearly needed; and it was in the autumn of 1912, after Picasso had left Sorgues, that Braque hit on the solution. He had been experimenting, during the summer, with scraps of folded newspaper; three-dimensional variants of the shapes in certain of his paintings—'free forms', one might say, for 'sculptures' is probably too august a word. If these forms could be, as it were, released out of the canvas and into the air, so could the paper take its place as a flat form within the picture: such would seem to have been the reasoning which crossed Braque's mind when he happened to see, in an Avignon shop-window, a piece of *trompe-l'oeil* wall-paper, printed to look like panelled oak. He bought a piece of this, took it home to Sorgues, and produced the picture which was one of the key-pieces in the great Braque exhibition of 1956 in Edinburgh and London. We can really only appreciate the originality of this picture if we remember the kind of painting which was most admired, in 1912, by the grandees of the day: the sumptuous Edwardian manipulations of paint, the dressed-up and high-lit fraudulence.

The *Fruit-Dish and Glass* which Braque drew and constructed in September 1912, is technically one of the most un-sumptuous pictures ever set before the public; it consists merely of a number of strips of wallpaper, cut and pasted on to a sheet of white paper, with a minimum of charcoal drawing to relate them to one another and to the composition as a whole. The drawn objects are: the bunch of grapes which had already appeared in one of Braque's experimental oil-and-sand pictures earlier that summer, an apple, and a glass. A table, a drawer, and a section of panelled wood are figured by the wallpaper. The words BAR and ALE traverse certain of the planes. In so far as, in this revolutionary work, the false has been made true (the 'imita-tion', i.e., been regenerated as a 'true' account of the experience of wood), the *Fruit-Dish and Glass* has an almost philosophical importance in the history of art. More empirically, it meant that 'real' matter could thenceforward be introduced into paintings. Not merely would such intruder-objects not be 'incongruous', but they would present an entirely new source of interplay between art and reality.

Braque was extremely scrupulous, not to say precautionary, in his use of the new method. Where Picasso's instinctive dynamism led him to an ever greater exuberance in the exploitation of the *papier collé*, Braque rarely used more than a telling minimum of charcoal drawing in any picture which included pasted paper; and, in general his *papiers collés* are tranquil, and at times even seraphic, in tone. Much of this is due to the fact that, for the first time in cubist painting, very large single planes are being employed. In analytical cubism, the planes had tended to be sharp-angled and suggestive of an intense nervous energy only just kept in control; in hermetic cubism, the spectator's powers of apprehension are working at their highest pressure in the effort to read the gnomic and congested canvas; but in the *papiers collés* which are the beginnings of synthetic cubism there are areas of great calm. The planes do not duck back and forth at a sharp angle; rather do they float unconcernedly at an angle of ninety degrees to the eye, as if knowing that the drawing, by turns shadowy and fugitive, incisive and exact, will indicate precisely their position in space. Artists have striven throughout history to provide a unique experience which cannot be counterfeited or experienced through any other means; and here, in the *papiers collés*

18

executed between September 1912 and the outbreak of war, Braque proves that this experience can be made up of the humblest of elements, and that those elements can turn out, by the intensity of their transformation, to have as great an effect upon us as any of the tours-de-force of *la belle peinture*. By 1913 a motor-car licence could be integrated with no sense of strain into the reclining oval of a synthetic cubist still-life.

Thus it came about that objects were literally 'disaffected' from their everyday significance; the permanence of meaning was destroyed at one stroke; and just as our conventional notion of space had been annihilated by analytical cubism, so was our notion of the identity of objects overthrown by synthetic cubism. The new procedure amounted, in short, to a synthetic reconstruction of reality; a reconstruction not built up, that is to say, from reality's original constituents but based on a heterogeneous assemblage of seemingly unrelated matter.

In Picasso's case, there seemed no limit to the heterogeneity of the elements which could be introduced into synthetic cubist pictures—or 'objects', as they would be better called, since often they turned out in the end to be more like reliefs, or sculptures, than two-dimensional paintings. Often, too, he brought to their fabrication a fiendish wit and unrestrained love of mischief which had no counterpart in Braque's fundamentally sober and ruminative methods of work. But what Braque did do was to ponder long and carefully how the new advantages of synthetic cubism could be incorporated into pure painting. At this point his mastery of counterfeit came into play; and two noble pictures reproduced in this book (17, 20) show to what effect he employed it, just as the collage still owned by Picasso (18) is one of many, dating from 1913, which illustrate the synthetic cubist device of operating on a basis (Mr. Cooper's phrase) of 'broad, thin, non-transparent planes of colour laid one over the other'. When this was transposed into oil-paint the result (17) displays on the one hand an unforced majesty of design, and on the other a diversity of texture which, when combined with incisive incidents of more or less naturalistic drawing, keeps our attention continually alert and presents us with a field of vision as varied and suggestive as any to be found in Nature.

What would have happened to Braque's work had the war not broken out in 1914 is a subject for lengthy speculation. Braque did not, for one reason or another, have much time to work in 1914, with the result that the enormously increased expressive possibilities of his art did not have time to work themselves out before he was called to the army in August of that year. But there are signs that he would have developed rather towards opulence and elaboration than towards a renewal of analysis. Even the broad flat planes of synthetic cubism were taking on a mottled or quasi-pointillist appearance; gesso and sawdust were getting into his paint; his colour was becoming richer and more assertive; the drawing of naturalistic detail had at times an epigrammatic quality; the 'imitation' patterning grew more and more elaborate, though the planes remained for the most part rectilinear; and although Braque could still put a tremendous 'punch' into the monumental figures-with-guitar that recalled the pioneering days of cubism, he had also begun to produce, in considerable numbers, an auxiliary *oeuvre* of accomplished minor pictures, ancestors of the cabinet-size still-lives which were to ingratiate themselves with so many collectors in the 1920s.

The collaboration between Picasso and Braque was broken off in August 1914, when Braque left for the war, and was never resumed. It is a partnership which has become one of the legends of art; but it could not in any case, I think, have lasted much longer, so great was the difference between the two natures involved and so brief the phase in their careers during which they could have worked together so closely. It must also be remembered that what had begun as a private adventure had become, by August 1914, a movement to which many were anxious to register themselves as adherents. Neither Braque nor Picasso had wished or intended to issue a *Discours de la Méthode*, where cubism was concerned; but there were plenty of people around who would have liked to formulate it for them. We know very well from Braque's notebooks what he thinks of them: 'Those who go on ahead have their backs to the people who follow—and that's all they deserve.' He knows, too, the difference between the painter who makes the initial effort and the follower whose role is, at best, that of consolidation. 'Raphael and Corot have something in common,' he once wrote, 'but Corot and Trouillebert have nothing in common, though there's a "likeness" between them.'

There was, all the same, one newcomer to the scene who had his own contribution to make. This was Juan Gris, who had developed very rapidly since he first began to paint seriously in 1911. So far from being one of what Braque called *les horribles serre-files*, Gris showed from the start a real independence of mind, seeking complexity when Braque and Picasso were 'flattening out' into a simpler kind of painting, heightening his colour when they would hardly touch anything but elephant-grey, and racing level with them when it came to exploiting the possibilities of collage.

That Gris had a personal veneration for Braque we know from many passages in his letters. In October 1914, when the first confusions of army life were still not resolved, he writes: 'I have no news of Braque, the person who interests me most.' And after Braque, then a 2nd Lieutenant, was wounded in the head at Carency in May 1915, it is through Gris that we have news of him; that he had kept from all his friends the fact that he was on the danger list, that he is going south (April 1916) for convalescence, that he seems to be throwing off the effects of trepanning, and that (January 1917) his friends have given a banquet to celebrate his return to Paris: 'It was charming, spirited, and full of good humour. Max Jacob at his most brilliant and witty in two parodies—one of a colonel, and the other of Braque's mother.'

It was, if anything, almost a source of relief to Gris that his admiration was later cooled by personal differences with Braque. ('I was so great an admirer of his painting,' he wrote in 1920, 'that I was being crushed by it.') But for our immediate purpose the striking fact is rather the extent to which, in the first important pictures he painted after being invalided out of the army, Braque drew near to Gris; notably in the *Woman with Mandoline* in the Dutilleul collection and the treatment of the hands, the guitar-strings, and the mask-like face in the monumental *Musician* (24).

About this latter picture there is a convalescent quality, an element of physical frailty in the long thin flat planes and the evident reluctance to step clear of the known world of synthetic-cubist practice. But, within those reservations, what a noble and original harmony is drawn from the colours! What elegance, what resource in the varieties of texture! And how distinguished, how *racé*, is the elongation of the forms! Beside this immensely sophisticated painting the *Man with Guitar* of 1914 looks almost brutish, and Picasso's *Man with Newspaper* of 1916 a monster of ebullience. The picture marks Braque's farewell both to pure synthetic-cubist idiom and to the figure-with-mandoline subject which served him so well since its first appearance in 1910.

One or two other pictures of this period bear witness to the way in which Braque could produce, even at this stage in his career, pictures whose complexity, refinement, and generally reminiscential character would normally call for the appellation 'late'. The *Guitar, Clarinet, and Bottle of Rum* of 1918, for instance (26), is a capital example of this, with *papier collé*, corrugated cardboard, gouache and charcoal all brought into play. But Braque is not a painter who luxuriates in the past, even though he likes, in kitchen-terms, to keep a good pot going and dip into it from time to time. Nor is he by nature a miniaturist, though nobody can produce more delectable small pictures when he turns his mind to it. From 1918 onwards his history has to be written more and more in terms of pictures as large in scope as they were in scale. And here two things must be said: one is that we have no Braque of this date and class in England, and the other is that reproduction, however conscientious, can only give a faint and partial idea of the majesty and originality of Braque's major works.

Braque was still only in his middle thirties when the war ended. But there is no doubt that his wound had left him, if not a 'changed' man, at any rate a man on whom suffering and enforced inactivity had left their mark. We

21

hear no more of the feats of colossal strength which so astonished his contemporaries in early youth; and in the maxims which he committed to paper from 1917 there is often the lapidary quality which comes from long and private meditation—and the use of that classic instrument of thought, the French language: what could be more succinct, for instance, than the aphorism 'Peindre n'est pas dépeindre'? And in another early maxim there is the essence of Braque's activity between 1917 and 1928: 'Nature,' he says, 'does not give us the taste for perfection. We cannot imagine her either better or worse.'

Braque had, in fact, reached the stage in his career at which he was able to begin thinking about whether his pictures were getting better or worse. Up to the 4th of August 1914, the basic problems were problems of kind; from 1917 onwards the idea of quality began to take over, since the question of kind had, broadly speaking, been settled once and for all. Take, for instance, the experiments with format which abound in the work of 1918-19: the diamond, the irregular oval, the parallelogram inset in a rectangle, the dark nutshell-outline that has floated to the top of a pale oblong, and so forth; all these relate to issues of presentation such as would never have occurred to Braque in the days when the problem of how to go on painting at all came uppermost. And with this new regard for presentation there came, inevitably, a greater concern with the purely painterly aspect of his art, a tendency to linger over the forms and invest them with a pictorial equivalent of *pourriture noble*, and a luxuriance of personal expression. These qualities were fused in a group of masterpieces dated 1918-19, several of which are reproduced in this book (25, 28, 29). The year 1919 also produced works like *The Sideboard* (27), in which Braque reverted to the flatter, less plastic methods of synthetic cubism; but in general the lyrical un-anchored style of *The Sideboard* was on the way out, in favour of the altogether more redoubtable manner of the *guéridon* series.

Although Picasso and Braque no longer saw much of one another there were still points of striking resemblance in their activity. Just as Braque's *Musician* of 1917-18 can be related to the Picasso *Man leaning on a Table* of 1915 (once owned by E. de Beaumont) by reason of the earlier picture's systematised use of tall thin vertical planes, so were Braque's massive *gueridons* paralleled by the *Still Life on a Guéridon* series, which Picasso began at Saint-Raphael in 1919. It seems possible that Picasso saw the three masterworks of this sort which Braque exhibited at Léonce Rosenberg's gallery in March 1919, just as Braque was undoubtedly fired, some ten years later, by the beach-scenes which Picasso painted at Dinard in 1928.

A painting like the *Café-Bar* of 1919 (29) explains why Juan Gris should have written, in September 1919, that 'Braque's experience begins to be considerable and now enables him to bring off some magnificent pictures';

for these were, in effect, triumphs of experience, re-workings on an ampler and more opulent scale of material already treated, for the most part, in earlier years. Their general plan remained strictly claustrophile (Braque did not use the open-window motif till 1938), but the device of the richly patterned floor, first mooted in *The Musician*, now bounces the eye well up into the powerfully worked-out central area; and in general the pictures give an impression of renewed energy and strength. Too much is going on in them for us to have any doubts as to the total recovery of Braque and his gifts. But there are, all the same, one or two smaller works of this period which are perhaps a little too relaxed in character, if we are to judge Braque by his own highest standards; we can understand why Gris should have called them, in February 1920, 'soft and lacking in precision'. Unluckily it is by work of this size and calibre that Braque is often judged, whereas the journey to Basle is well repaid by the sight of the *Café-Bar* in which Braque added to the flat overlapping planes of synthetic cubism a new fullness and amplitude of colour.

That Braque has strong views on certain frailties we may judge from the observation in his notebooks that 'All Joffre was concerned with in 1914 was to do Vernet's battle-pieces all over again'. And in 1921 and 1922 he was outraged in a more directly professional matter: the sale, by order of the French Government, of Kahnweiler's entire stock of paintings. (Technically an enemy alien from 1914 to 1918, Kahnweiler had had his stock-in-trade confiscated.) This was doubly galling to Braque, in that his own dealer, Léonce Rosenberg, presided over sales at which many of his finest pictures were sold for relatively little, just when he was beginning to command reasonable prices. As little as 230 francs was paid for some of his smaller canvases; and it is understandable that Braque should have given way to his feelings by giving Léonce Rosenberg a blow in the face when the pictures were put on view at the Hôtel Drouot.

These disturbances did not, however, communicate themselves to Braque's work, which was marked early in 1922 by the beginnings of an entirely new vein: that of the monumental figure-paintings of which the best-known are the 'Basket-Bearers' or *Canephorae* (32, 37). Initially as nearly two-dimensional as the majestic forms would allow, the series later took on, as in the *Nude with Basket of Fruit* of 1924, now at Santa Barbara, California, an element almost of romantic drama, with something of traditional chiaroscuro in the presentation of the head; and the *Recumbent Nude* of the same year, now in the Chester Dale collection, could be a free version of one of Tintoretto's small panels. These pictures form, in short, a complex and ambiguous series, and it will not quite do to say, as several fine judges have said, that the figures have a neutral character and do not exploit the sensual aspect of the naked female body. It would be a narrow view of

23

sensuality that did not recognise the erotic potentialities that slumber within these giantesses. It cannot have been by accident that when Braque came, in 1931-32, to illustrate an ancient classic at Vollard's invitation, the poem in question was Hesiod's *Theogony*. Nor do we need to seek out that rare and costly book for an authentic image of Hesiod's heroines, the 'immortal goddesses who lay with mortal men and bore them children like unto gods'; 'all-nourishing Demeter' could be the subject of more than one of Braque's pastels of 1922-23, just as the vast frame of the basket-bearer in the Washington National Gallery might well represent 'wide-bosomed Earth, the ever-sure foundation of all'. And there are other seated nudes of 1924 and 1925 in which only a puny imagination could fail to find some reflection of 'member-loving Aphrodite'.

But what *is* true is that it is not in these pictures that the voluptuous elements in Braque's nature are most clearly evident. Where Braque excels is in the use of a distributed sensuality; and it was in the early 1920s that he first began to combine, to such marvellous effect, the sensuality of the marks on the canvas with the sensuality of the thing remembered. Originally he had striven to dissociate or disaffect the one from the other. Objects had entered his pictures only when purified of their everyday connotation; and the impermanence of 'meaning', as it is generally understood, had been, as it is again today, a fundamental part of Braque's belief. 'No object,' as he lately said to John Richardson, 'can be tied down to any one sort of reality.' But the look and the feel of things *is* 'one sort of reality'; and Braque tried, from the early 1920s onwards, to realise that look and feel as fully as was possible within the complex architecture of his major works. These intentions he realised to splendid effect in the great series of *cheminées* (33), in the *Marble Table* in the Musée d'Art Moderne (36) in Paris, and in many smaller pieces of 1922-25.

First mooted in an analytical-cubist composition of 1911, the theme of the chimney-piece had the advantage that it presented, by definition, the shallow picture-space which made it easy for him to bring all the objects within touching-distance; and, with this, it offered both a complex and original architectural design and many built-in contrasts of texture. All these he combined to magisterial effect in a group of paintings where he tried 'to see how far he could go in an alliance between volume and colour'. It is in connection with this period, when objects were allowed in with, as it were, their personalities complete and fully rounded, that Chardin's name is so often invoked. In point of fact many of Braque's small cabinet-pictures are arguably nearer to Oudry in stature and intention; and, apart from this, there is in Braque's character a strain of philosophical ambition and a liking for vast and audacious formal undertakings which are quite lacking in Chardin. But when Braque allows his tenderness full play, as in nos. 31 and

35, then truly we are reminded of how Chardin put before us 'the shaggy velvet of the peach, the amber transparency of the white grape, the sugary rime of the plum, the moist crimson of strawberries, the hardy berry of the muscatel and its smoke-blue film, the wrinkles and tubercles of an orange-skin, the embroidered guipure of melons, the copperas of old apples, the knots in a crust of bread, the smooth rind of the chestnut and the wood of the hazel nut. All this is placed before you in the light, in the atmosphere, within reach, as it might be, of your hand.'

Chardinesque, likewise, is Braque's way of ennobling the most familiar household objects—the napkin in its ring, for instance—and of course Braque's fondness for the long oblong format can be related to that used by Chardin, for much the same purposes, in his *Attributes of the Arts* in Leningrad. The comparison can, even so, be overdone; and in the stern inner logic which was responsible for Braque's change of style in the second half of the 1920s there is a quality quite personal to Braque.

Once again it is possible to interpret these changes as a delayed reaction to work done by Picasso some years earlier. Certainly in the large and brilliant still-lives done by Picasso—at Juan-les-Pins in 1924, above all—there is a quality, at once ruthless, festive and alert, which contrasts very strongly with those cabinet-pieces by Braque where the forms run like honey and the gamut of colour is, on the whole, passive and subdued. Already in the *Marble Table* (36) of 1925 Braque had aimed to combine an extremely voluptuous paint-quality—and when Braque paints marble it seems to be one of the most suggestive substances in Nature—with a renewed energy in the manhandling of the other elements in the design. By 1927, when he painted the *Black Rose* (38), the deliquescence of the early 1920s had given place to a firmer and more masculine handling: this we note in the division into dark and light of many of the component objects, in the restriction of patterning to that element (the cloth) in which it appears 'naturally', and in the use of silhouette and emphasised outline to situate the objects in space. Braque went on to abandon, very largely, the vocabulary of fullness and ripeness which had won him so many admirers. Now that the heaviness of things no longer greatly concerned him, he began to situate them in space with a marvellous freedom and address; and colour, likewise dissociated from any obligation to volume, became lighter and sharper and more inventive. A new energy began to course through the pictures; and by 1929, when he painted the *Round Table* (44), Braque's imagination was functioning in a manner at once fanciful and august and his paint, though less rich than five years earlier, seemed to have thinned down the better to communicate the pressure and inspiration of the painter's ideas. In the Chester Dale *Le Jour* of the same period (43), the wall is still treated mainly as a source of ornamental pattern, the table-top, legs and drawer as a pretext for *trompe-l'oeil* graining, and the panelling as a device for the introduction of those strong plain verticals which, as in the *cheminée* series, are used to hold the still-life in place. The picture-space remains very shallow. But in the *Round Table* all this has changed: elements of traditional perspective thrust back into the picture-space, leaving the air free to penetrate round the table; a multiple viewpoint turns the ceiling into an agglomeration of dipping and overlapping planes; there are no *trompe-l'oeil* patternings to tease the eye away from the majestic, free-running outlines. Braque's imagination seems to work, here, at so great a heat that the idea of fidgeting with ornamentation could not be entertained. (Even the pedestal takes on the dignity of Romanesque arching.) There is, however, a characteristic carry-over of fancy in the fact that the motif of music, everywhere present in the still-life, recurs even in the dado, where the scroll-device reminds us of the sound hole in a violin. Braque delights in such 'rhymes'.

The *Round Table* is, all the same, something of a sport among Braque's major works. By the following year, as we see in the *Bottle of Marc* (45), he was practising a style nearer to the *Musician* of 1917, although the planes have a far greater variety of shape and direction and the oppositions of colour and texture are subtler and more expert. The resource displayed in this largely synthetic-cubist picture is such that Braque may well have felt that nothing more could be done in that style. Certainly he was at that time pondering the possibilities of line as the new dominant factor in his work. Of the effects of this notion, much evidence is to hand: etchings for Hesiod (1931-32), incisions on plaster of figures from Greek mythology (46, 47), beach-scenes (48) inspired, it may be, by the acquisition in 1929 of a summer-house at Varengeville, near Dieppe, and a group of recumbent nudes. In some of these paintings there are passages of savage distortion, re-inventions of the kind put about by Picasso between 1927 and 1929, which are difficult to tie in with our normal experience of Braque; and therefore it is usual to say that both in these cases and in the *Woman's Head* of 1930 and the *Seated Musician* of 1931 Braque for once 'does not arrive at a convincing personal idiom'.

These curious works do none the less have a bearing upon the masterpieces of Braque's old age. He takes away, to begin with, the beauty of paint, the contrasts of texture and ornamentation, and the elaborations of structure which mark the great still-lives of 1927-30; in their place we find washes of thin paint, subdued colour dissociated from the enigmatic and curvilinear drawing, and something monstrous and equivocal in the characterisation of, for instance, the figures which recline or strangely prance upon the hutted beach. Quite apart from the erotic connotations of some of these paintings, they demonstrate, I think, the point made by Braque in conversation with Mr. Richardson when he said: 'It is the act of painting, not the finished product, which counts. I never know how a painting is going to develop. For instance, I sometimes find myself starting a picture as a figure composition and finishing it as a still-life.' And there are, in effect, still-lives of this period which are almost identical in lay-out, wash-structure, and arabesque with pictures in the *Bathers* series. When Mr. Richardson describes the large *Billiard Table* of fifteen years later as achieving 'a perfect pictorial harmony by virtue of the liberties he has taken not so much with the appearances as with the identities of things' he speaks of a procedure first mooted in the experimental paintings of the early 1930s.

Some part of Braque's restlessness at this period may have been due to the imminence of his first major retrospective exhibition, which was held at the Kunsthalle in Basle in April 1933. Such an ordeal can be particularly disquieting for an artist who, like Braque, paints entirely for himself and tends never to show his work if he can help it. But the Basle exhibition confirmed his position as one of the major masters of the day, and it was followed in July 1934 by an exhibition in London, at Messrs. Reid & Lefevre. There were forty-one items in the catalogue, Braque came over for the occasion, and the prices (from £55 upwards) were almost laughably low by the standards of today. The emphasis was on Braque's more recent work, and to that extent we might not now think it ideally representative; but work of all periods was on show and there were at least half a dozen major paintings. In all four pictures were sold: the two more important ones to dealers. No English connoisseur was prepared to go above £120 for a Braque, and the press-cutting book, which the Directors were kind enough to show me, is a *sottisier* worthy of Flaubert. Even the most enlightened of English critics treated Braque as a painter of only intermittent individuality, and warned his readers that the incised plasters 'will need some study and much good will if they are to be enjoyed'. For an estimate of Braque that chimes with our own we should have to go back ten years—and, admittedly, to a phase in which he was more accessible: to December 1924, when Sickert said in the *Burlington Magazine* that 'Braque is occupied with quality, and finds salvation in a delicate and exquisite economy of means. Such learned execution confers a sort of magical interest on whatever he touches.'

As if in instinctive reaction against the incised line, sparse furnishing and generally gnomic procedures of 1931-33, Braque reverted towards the end of 1933 to an altogether more sumptuous and elaborate style. For one reason or another he saw, quite literally, *la vie en rose* in such canvases as the *Pink Cloth* of 1933; and in the *Yellow Cloth* of 1935, which won first prize at the Carnegie Exhibition in Pittsburg in 1937, the orchestration matches pallor for pallor in a way which is, even for him, astonishingly adroit. But, as we can see in the *Still Life with Mandoline* of 1935-38 (51) his art was once again on the move. In certain respects—the use of the dado, for instance, and

27

of the corkscrew legs to steady the composition, the imitation graining, and the all-but-vertical hoop of the table-top, it harks back to earlier pictures on the same theme. But whereas, in the 20s, Braque would probably have allowed each component in the picture its own identity, and might at some periods have modelled it fully to that end, here the composition takes charge: most of the objects are flattened, some are distorted in order not to disturb the 'run' of the composition, and the picture as a whole is marked by a *horror vacui* not entirely explained by the fact that the picture was intended to serve as a tapestry design. The immediate purpose of the ornamentation is, as Braque has said, to 'liberate colour from form'; and the subordination of the objects to the *tempo primo* of the composition represents one aspect of the problem which Braque was to solve so brilliantly in the great series of post-war *Studios*. Over the last twenty years Braque has, in fact, attacked the problem of the identity of objects in two antithetical ways: on the one hand, by allowing *la belle peinture* its revenge and treating the objects in his cabinet-pictures with a fullness and an expressive power which have no rival in modern times; and, on the other, by ignoring, or over-ruling, or so transposing that identity that, as he says, 'a new destiny' befalls the objects in question and they are caught up, as in the *Studios*, in a vast ordered commotion in which the idea of everyday 'meaning' is suspended.

Not, of course, that this development could be foretold from the still-lives of the 1930s; but, now that we know to what these pictures were leading, we can see that already in the very large *Still Life with Mandoline* of 1938 there is present what we might call the magical element in Braque's post-war handling of space: this it is which persuades us to accept as logical what are, in fact, arbitrary manipulations of the objects concerned and, eventually, to suspend our usual notion of the weight, the movement, and the hierarchy of objects in space.

In 1936 Braque began a new series of figure-compositions: or, more exactly, interiors in which figures play an articulative part. Plates 52 and 53 reproduce two of the less elaborate of these: in both the figure is seen at once from the front and from the side, and there are elements on the one hand of naturalistic drawing and circumstantial detail and, on the other, of distortion for rhythmic and compositional reasons. In plate 52 the dark side of the head clearly harks back to the incised plasters with which Braque had been experimenting, and in plate 53 there is in the drawing and set of the hat a close attention to details of fashion which situates the picture more exactly in time than is usual for Braque. In both pictures the lighter side of the torso is treated in the free, billowy style which recurs also in the familiar *Duet* of 1937 in the Musée d'Art Moderne in Paris. In some of the more elaborate works in this series there are episodes of extraordinary beauty; still-life passages, pictures within the picture, and occasionally, as in the

Studio with Still Life of 1938, a resurgence of erotic feeling. But in general these are transitional and somewhat uneasy pictures, in which we sense that the artist has a great deal more to say and is feeling round for the best way to say it.

(On the compositional level, for instance, one symptom of the struggle towards a new range of expression is the fact that Braque tended in several important pictures to discard the principle of the central figure, or central knot of interest, which had governed so many of his canvases, in favour of forms balanced to left and right of a central axis. In this there may have been a harking back to earlier inspirations: to Cézanne, for instance, in that Braque's *Duet* of 1937 has obvious similarities to the *Ouverture de Tann-hauser* in the Hermitage.)

A premonitory picture, in this connection, is the *Studio* of 1939 (55), an untenanted interior in which Braque once again did not base the composition upon a central point of interest. He put, instead, the still-life of flowers well away to the left; to the right he had his easel, and on it was the first of the bird-images which were to flap or float through so many of his later works; in the middle was a window, with certain meteorological indications to be detected through the panes; and much of the lower half of the canvas was taken up with a sort of fence of tall flat thin vertical planes, with a great variety of imitation wood-graining. Just 'in front' of these planes were the painter's palette and a rustic stool, once again portrayed in terms of *trompe-l'oeil* grained wood and wicker-work. This picture now seems to us both a beginning and an end: an end, in that the flattened forms, the tall flat planes, and the deliberate variations of texture are a last manifestation of devices which Braque had originated twenty years earlier; and a beginning, in that the picture is a ranging-shot for the great symphonic interiors of 1949-56 in which Braque walls himself up inside his studio and makes of it a place for which we would gladly forsake the world outside.

The point of the great *Studio* series is that it combines both a private *poétique* and the results of a lifetime of experimentation with the handling of objects in space. What objects are chosen, and how they are combined—these are Braque's private concerns; but the manner in which reality is re-discovered has implications far beyond the workings, however fertile, of an individual imagination. The choice of the studio as subject is easily ex-plained: a studio is, first of all, a place in which strange conjunctions of objects are always to be expected; like the quays of Le Havre, where Braque walked as a boy, they are rich in juxtapositions odder and more suggestive than those offered by any ordinary interior. Second, a painter's studio is one of the few holy places in which we still whole-heartedly believe; it has a status half-workshop, half-temple of Dionysus. Georges Limbour describes, for instance, how when he went to Braque's studio at

Varengeville he was greeted with the words: 'Well, this is where it all goes on!' 'What was that *it*?' Limbour goes on to ask: 'That something not easily named or explained which went on uninterruptedly, unendingly, with such absolute constancy, all day and all night?' And, of course, Braque is not going to answer the question for us: 'The only thing that matters in art,' he wrote in his notebooks, 'is what cannot be explained.'

Braque might, no doubt, have pressed on more rapidly towards the definitive *Studios* had it not been for the outbreak of war in September 1939. When the Germans overran Holland and Belgium in May 1940 he left Varengeville and headed south, not to return to Normandy till September 1944. For a time it must have seemed as if not only the *Studio* project but the studio itself was doomed. But in the autumn of 1940 he returned to the house in Paris which had been built for him by Auguste Perret in 1924; and there he remained for the rest of the war, with German officers in the house across the road and a succession of proposals, both from Vichy and the Germans, all of which, unlike some of his painter-colleagues, he turned down. And, in spite of the difficulties and discouragements of the day, he went on working.

Some of the pictures were based, as had long been his custom, on themes already mooted: the *Jug and Skull* of 1943, for instance, combines the high-beaked jug, familiar from other paintings, with the skull which formed part of the *Vanitas* of 1939. ('A skull has a beautiful structure,' he once remarked, 'and it's used to waiting.') In the elaborate and luxurious *Patience* of 1942 Braque reverses the composition he had devised for the *Woman with a Mandolin* of 1937; and, in the same fruitful year, he produced one of the most popular of all his paintings, the *Black Fishes*, now in the Musée d'Art Moderne in Paris, and the large *Interior*, now in the de Menil collection, Houston, U.S.A., in which he renewed the enquiries last adumbrated in the *Studio* of 1939.

In some of these pictures the innate dandyism of Braque's procedures comes marvellously to the fore. To the mackerel, as later to the portly outline of the John Dory, he gave a distinction which these creatures can rarely have enjoyed. When the overladen buffets of the 20s were no longer to hand he turned to the debris of bathroom and kitchen: the worn hairbrush, the substitute for soap, the ragged towel; and from these, as from the radiator, the dishcloth, the tall-funneled stove, the coal-bucket and the single onion he drew what was, for him, a new kind of poetry, with the paint loosely and at times almost roughly applied. Bad weather lowered at the open window; and although Braque was still capable (as in the *Jug, Glass and Lemons* of 1942) of cabinet-pictures as delectable as any he had ever painted, the general tone of his work at that time was understandably overcast. (In the square *Red Guéridon* of 1942, where the intention was presumably festive, the note is quite clearly forced). Something of this sombreness persisted right through the war and indeed well into 1945: the wrenched-about drawing and heavily impasted background of the *Green Tablecloth* (61) were even more accentuated in such still-lives of 1944 as *The Pumpkin* and *The Sickle*, where both sickle and pumpkin are treated almost with hatred and the background looks as if powdered coal or slag had been mixed into the paint. And there is a magisterial dejection in the tall thin *Bathroom with Green Checks* of 1945.

If these autobiographical pictures now strike us forcibly it is because the general tone of Braque's work is one of such golden moderation. His is, we feel, a nature too powerful, too robust, too much in harmony with itself to submit for long to terrestrial inconvenience. And, in effect, Braque did recover remarkably well both from the war and from the serious illnesses which befell him in 1945 and 1947. (On the latter occasion his friend Nicolas de Staël probably saved his life by getting him into the American Hospital at Neuilly.) But even when he began, with the promise of better times, to tackle more complex and ambitious subjects, there lingered certain souvenirs of the dismal years. Take the *Billiard-Table* of 1945 (63), for instance. The notion of hingeing the table in space and folding the whole composition around a vertical line some way to the right of the centre of the picture is one of the most audacious and fruitful that Braque had had for some time; (the wraith-like outlines in the foreground stand for the painter's easel and are seen also in the de Menil *Interior* of 1942); but the furnishing of the picture—the diamond-lattice of the windows, the undecorated walls, the wooden moulding with its natural ugliness unredeemed and none of the beauty which the Braque of an earlier day would have wrung from it—all this is stamped '1945': even the still-life of flowers is a sad spiky affair. In another billiard-picture, now in a Mexican collection, Braque takes the table head-on, with the hinge, this time, horizontally, across its middle and reversed perspective to bring the far end within reach of the observer. The tall composition stands on the table's sturdy legs, just like a still-life of the 1920s; there is a *trompe-l'oeil* coat-hanger to the right at the top; the electric-light fittings are noted down with Braque's wartime eye; and to the left there is what looks, from photographs, to be a telephone receiver: altogether a complex, amply-furnished and variously-textured picture—but one, be it noted, which Braque began in 1944 and did not complete until 1952, by which time he and the world were in very different shape.

If Braque's wartime paintings were in many cases autobiographical, in an anecdotal sense, the *Studios* of 1949-56 are autobiographical in a sense altogether more august; their subject-matter is, in fact, Braque's private universe, treated both circumstantially, in that nearly all their paraphernalia may actually be found in his studios, and philosophically, in that they set out

31

his definitive views on the problem which has preoccupied him all his working life: how best, and in what style, to represent the inside of a room. And,
as always, Braque is a master of the co-existence of these two aspects of the
matter. (When, for instance, he suggests in the *Studios* that space is neither
flat, nor round, nor rectangular, nor basin-shaped, but corrugated, we
remember that on his work-table the pencils lie assembled on a large sheet
of corrugated paper.)

The *Studios* have, in addition, a third subject: what I have described above
as 'the impermanence of meaning'. It is here, as much as in the arbitrary
management of space, that Braque's *poétique* resides. The enormous bird
takes off from the canvas on the easel and flies through the room; an arrow-
head, the word CAHIER, and a cog-wheel take their places in the composition as if by right, though it is impossible to account in logic for their
arrival; and, more than this, the look, substance, feel, and function of objects
and forms are metamorphosed without ever causing us to doubt that these
are, in the end, representations of reality.

Not all the *Studios* are equally complex; in no. 1 (65), for instance,
Braque comes as near as he would ever allow to a feat of unmotivated
virtuosity; the two unrelated canvases and the strip of ponderous gilded
frame make up what is, in effect, rather a cabinet-picture, consummately
spare and adroit, than a member of the great experimental series. By the
time Braque reached no. 5, on the other hand (66), the autobiographical
element was enhanced by, among other things, the apparition of, to the left,
the okapi-legged table which figures in one of the freshest and most elegant
of his later pictures, the *Still-Life on a Guéridon* of 1939-52. Colour had been
almost entirely subdued, as in the crucial days of cubism, and it was not until
no. 8 in the series was reached that vermilion, strontian yellow and pale
green began to lighten the colour-construction. (The priming of the
picture is grey, whereas the previous seven had a black priming.)

These are difficult pictures, certainly; but not so difficult that we cannot
find on almost every hand features that lead us back into Braque's earlier
work. In the foreground, for instance, we remember how from his earliest
days Braque would put an architectural feature or a fragment of still-life
almost into the observer's lap in order to make sure that he got into the
picture, as it were, on Braque's own terms. And the household apparatus:
the plain screens, the jars that swell to the size of amphorae, the elaborately
individualised electric fittings, the classicising heads from Braque's own
hand and the odd bits of 'sculpture' to which he has given house-room—all
these can be picked out as surely in the *Studios* as in photographs of one or
other of Braque's studios. Even the deliberately varied and manipulated
light of the south-facing studios seems destined to serve pictures such as
these; and it is also significant, I am sure, that when Braque came to the

ninth and last of the *Studios* he did not choose one of the formats for whose renewal he is famous—the *dessus de portes* or *chutes d'armes* of the twentieth century—but that most taxing of shapes, the square. By the choice of this format, which he had essayed on a smaller scale in the *Woman with Hat* of 1937 and the beautiful *Packing-Case* of 1948, Braque proved once again that his plan of campaign, like Turenne's, becomes ever more audacious with age. We cannot but admire a painter who concedes so little, in his seventies, to the charms of acceptable repetition. But we know how strong are his views on the dangers of habit; 'the artist's personality does not consist,' he once wrote, 'in the ensemble of his tics.' And when we think that these mysterious and complex works were given to the world at a time Braque was at last enjoying the reputation he deserves, we also remember the advice he gave to de Stael: that 'painting is an answer to everything—even success.'

The esoteric grandeur of the *Studios* has understandably deflected attention from the many less obviously 'important' paintings which Braque has also completed in recent years. But no aspect of his golden old age is negligible: neither the prints published by the Galerie Maeght, nor the reliefs in painted plaster (72), nor the handsome and costly illustrated books, nor the re-workings of earlier pictures (69), nor the flower-pieces, nor the manipulations of the bird-images (76, 79, 80) which figure both in some of the *Studios* and in the ceiling-panels painted in 1952-53 for the Etruscan Room in the Louvre.

Above all the late landscapes have, I think, had less than their due. For anything comparable to the *Birds* of 1957 (77) we should have to go back to the pictures painted by Van Gogh at Auvers in the last weeks of his life—with the distinction, however, that where Van Gogh's birds are creatures of ill-omen, like the *Krähe* in 'Die Winterreise', Braque's are bumbly old black biplanes, Blériot-birds such as must have hovered over the countryside when Braque was a young man. Braque in his middle seventies can do anything he likes with paint, and at times, as in the *Seascape* of 1953 (71), the paint is suave, Whistlerian almost, in its fluidity. But these relaxed and milky textures are exceptional; more commonly the late landscapes are marvels of concentrated vehemence, in which we cannot but admire the intensity of expression within the tiny compass, the exact analysis of the look and feel of the Normandy countryside, and the eloquent commotion of the touchable paint. In earlier landscapes, such as the *Boats on the Beach* of 1929 (41) Braque displays an eye for scenic effect which may have been sharpened by his experience as scene-designer for the ballets of Diaghilev and Etienne de Beaumont; certainly these paintings would 'tell' to admiration if they were enlarged to serve as drop-curtains. Elsewhere Braque pulls the facts of landscape this way and that in the interests of visual punning; and there are gratuitous elegances of texture, as when, in the *Boats under the Cliffs* of 1938, in the collection of the late E. C. Gregory, he turned the stones on the beach into enormous grains of caviar. Delectable as these pictures often are, they give no foretaste of the gravity of the late landscapes; rarely in art have such 'little' pictures been packed with so much meaning, so much experience, so wise an understanding of the possibilities of paint.

Among the larger late paintings the *Ajax* of 1949-54, now in the Marx collection, Chicago, was quick to become famous. Forecast by, among other things, a tinted engraving dated 'c. 1934' by Maurice Gieure in his book on Braque's drawings, it presents a lifesize evocation of the great warrior and is the metamorphosis, *en noble* and in masculine terms, of the dart-headed tennis-players of 1932 and the arabesques of the Hesiod series. Where the line had had (in the *Herakles*, of 1932, for instance) a tentative, cottony character, it is here as decisive as it is economical. It is as if Braque had harked back to his athletic youth and bodied forth an ideal image of supple and triumphant manhood. We see Ajax in the very act of driving out of the picture the adversary whose leg appears in the lower right half of the canvas, and it is notable that Braque has added to his original design the bow which his hero holds in his left hand. (If we compare the late *Chariot of the Sun* (72) with the *Io* etching in the 'Theogony' we shall find, I think, a comparable gain in nervous élan.)

To produce new marvels in old age is the dream of many an artist, but few realise that dream as completely as Dr. Braque (for so we may now style him, since Oxford University has conferred on him an Honorary Doctorate). If there were ever a danger of his repeating himself, he met that danger squarely and drove it, as would his Ajax, clean 'out of the picture'. And just as there is nothing in his late work for which excuses need be made, so has nothing in his own actions ever detracted from the dignity and privacy of the image of him which arises in the mind after prolonged study of his work. He personifies the classic French virtues in an age when France seems largely to have forsaken them; and when we remember the frailties from which even the major painters of our day are not always exempt—the bigotry in religion, the egregious political blunders, and the craving for publicity, no matter how inane—we must respect Braque the more for having shown us that a great painter can also be, and remain, *un grand monsieur*.

THE PLATES

THE PLATES

I THE MAST, ANTWERP. 1906

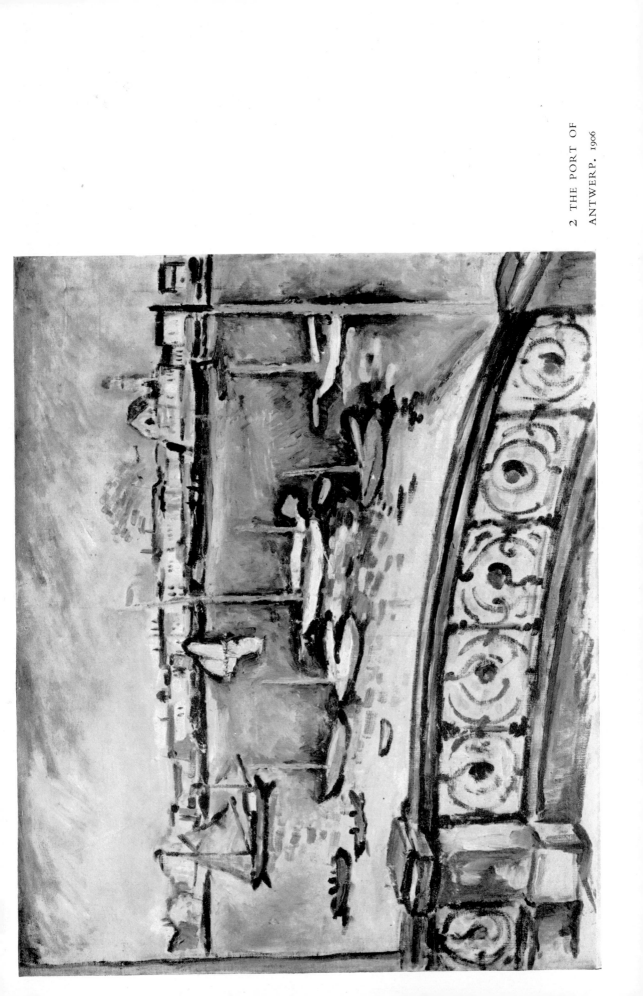

4 LANDSCAPE AT
L'ESTAQUE. 1906

5 THE PORT OF
LA CIOTAT. 1907

6 HOUSES AT L'ESTAQUE. 1908

7 LANDSCAPE AT L'ESTAQUE. 1908

8 THE PORT. 1908

9 LA ROCHE-GUYON: THE CASTLE. 1909

10 PIANO AND GUITAR. 1909-10

11 VIOLIN AND JUG. 1910

12 YOUNG GIRL, HALF-LENGTH. About 1910

13 THE PORTUGUESE. 1911

14 THE GUÉRIDON. 1911-12

15 STILL LIFE WITH VIOLIN. 1912.

16 COMPOSITION WITH ACE OF CLUBS. 1912-13

17 WOMAN WITH GUITAR. 1913

18 GUITAR AND
CINEMA
PROGRAMME. 1913

20 GLASS AND VIOLIN. 1913-14

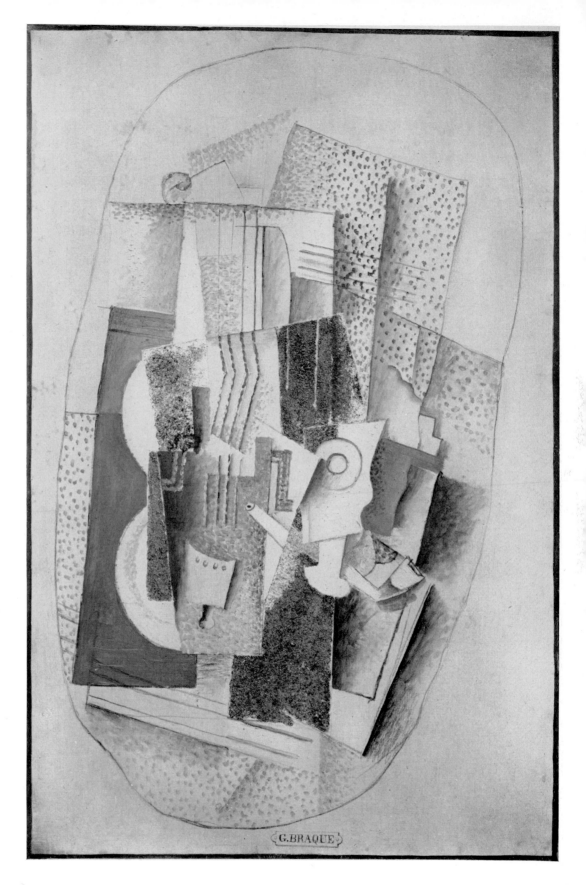

21 MUSIC. 1914

24 THE MUSICIAN. 1917-18

25 THE GUÉRIDON. 1918

27 THE SIDEBOARD. 1919

28 STILL LIFE ON A MANTELPIECE. 1919

29 CAFÉ BAR. 1919

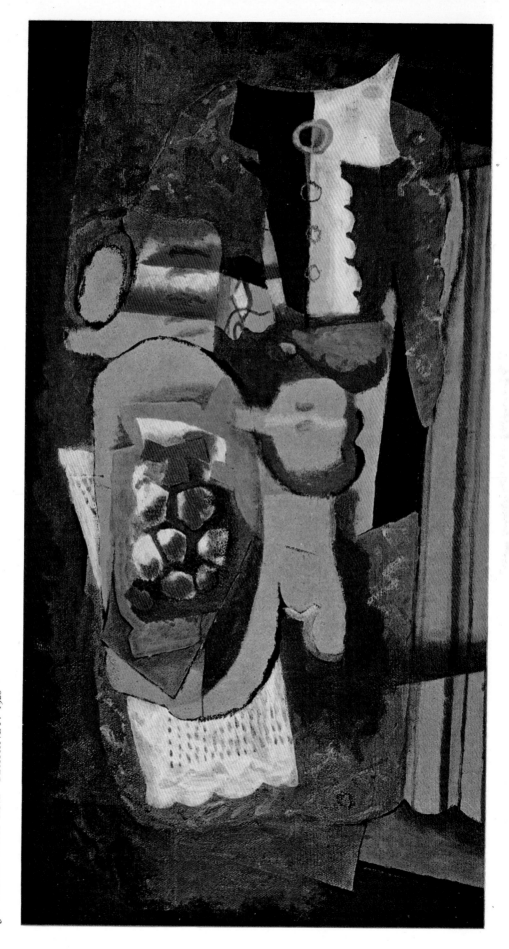

31 FRUIT DISH AND CLARINET. 1920

32   CANEPHORUS. Two Pendants. 1922

33 THE MANTELPIECE. 1922

34 FRUIT, JUG AND PIPE. 1924

35 GLASS AND PORCELAIN BOWL. 1924

36 THE MARBLE TABLE. 1925

37 NUDE WITH BASKET OF FRUIT. 1926

38 THE BLACK ROSE. 1927

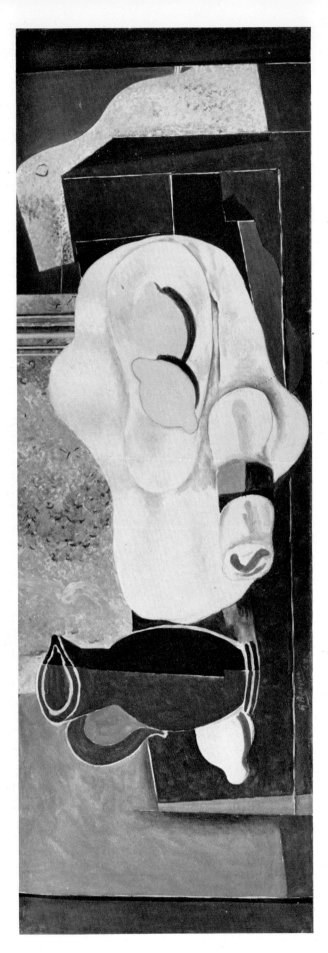

40 LEMONS AND NAPKIN RING. 1928

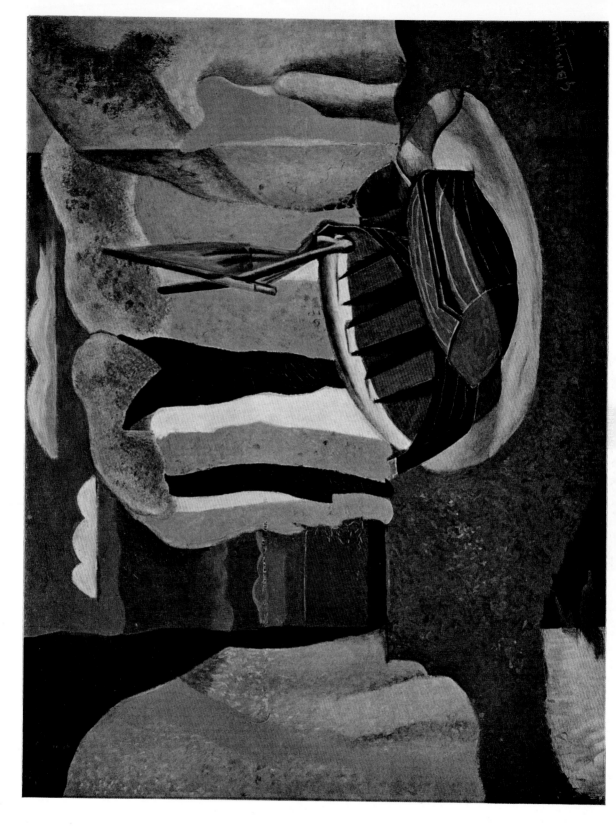

41 BOATS ON THE
BEACH: DIEPPE. 1929

42 STILL LIFE. 1929

43 STILL LIFE: LE JOUR.
1929

44 THE ROUND TABLE. 1929

45 THE BOTTLE OF MARC. 1930

46 ZELOS, NIKE. Incised Plaster, 1931

47 HERAKLES. Incised Plaster, 1931.

50   STILL   LIFE.   1934

51 STILL LIFE WITH
MANDOLINE. 1935

52 WOMAN PAINTING. 1936

53 WOMAN WITH HAT. 1937

54 GRAPES AND FLOWERS.

1934-39

56 INTERIOR WITH PALETTE. 1941

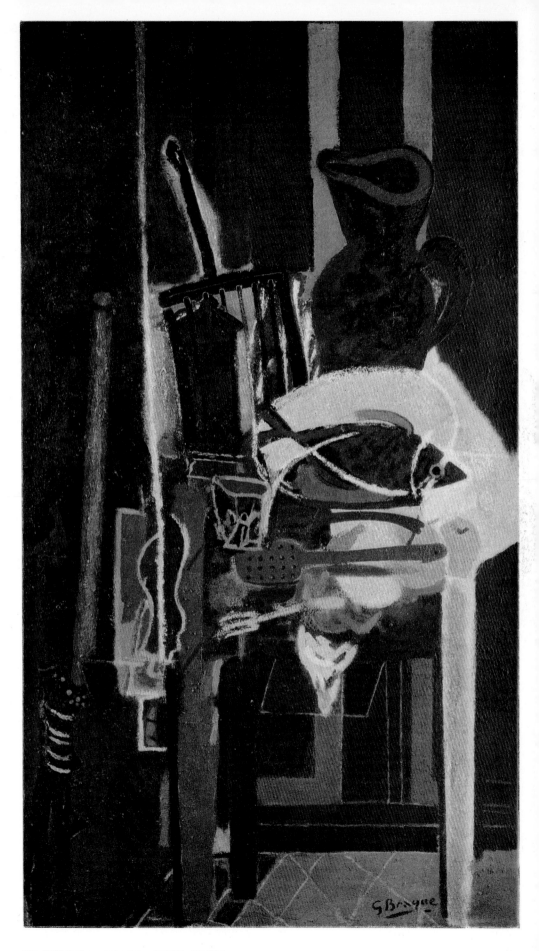

57 KITCHEN TABLE WITH GRILL. 1942

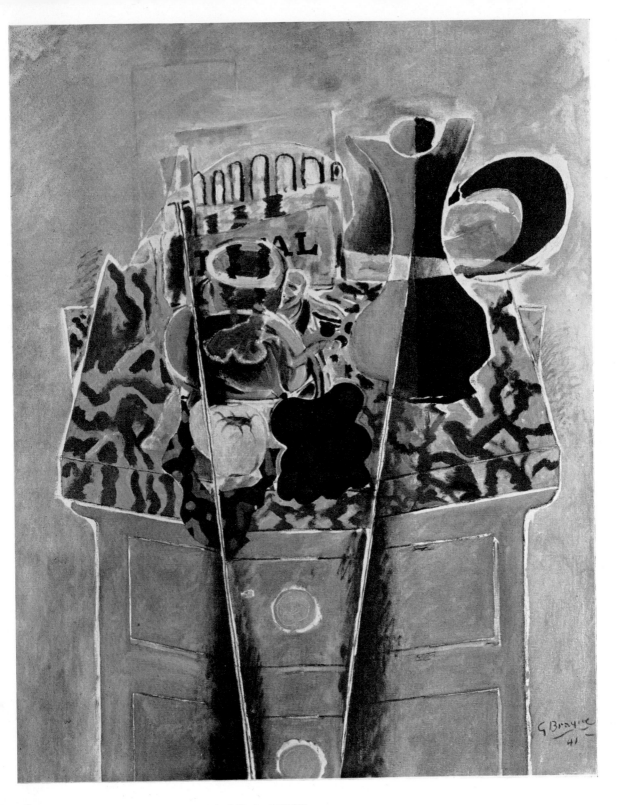

58 BUNCH OF GRAPES AND JUG ON A CHEST. 1941

59 THE PINK GUÉRIDON. 1942

60 FISH AND DECANTER. 1943

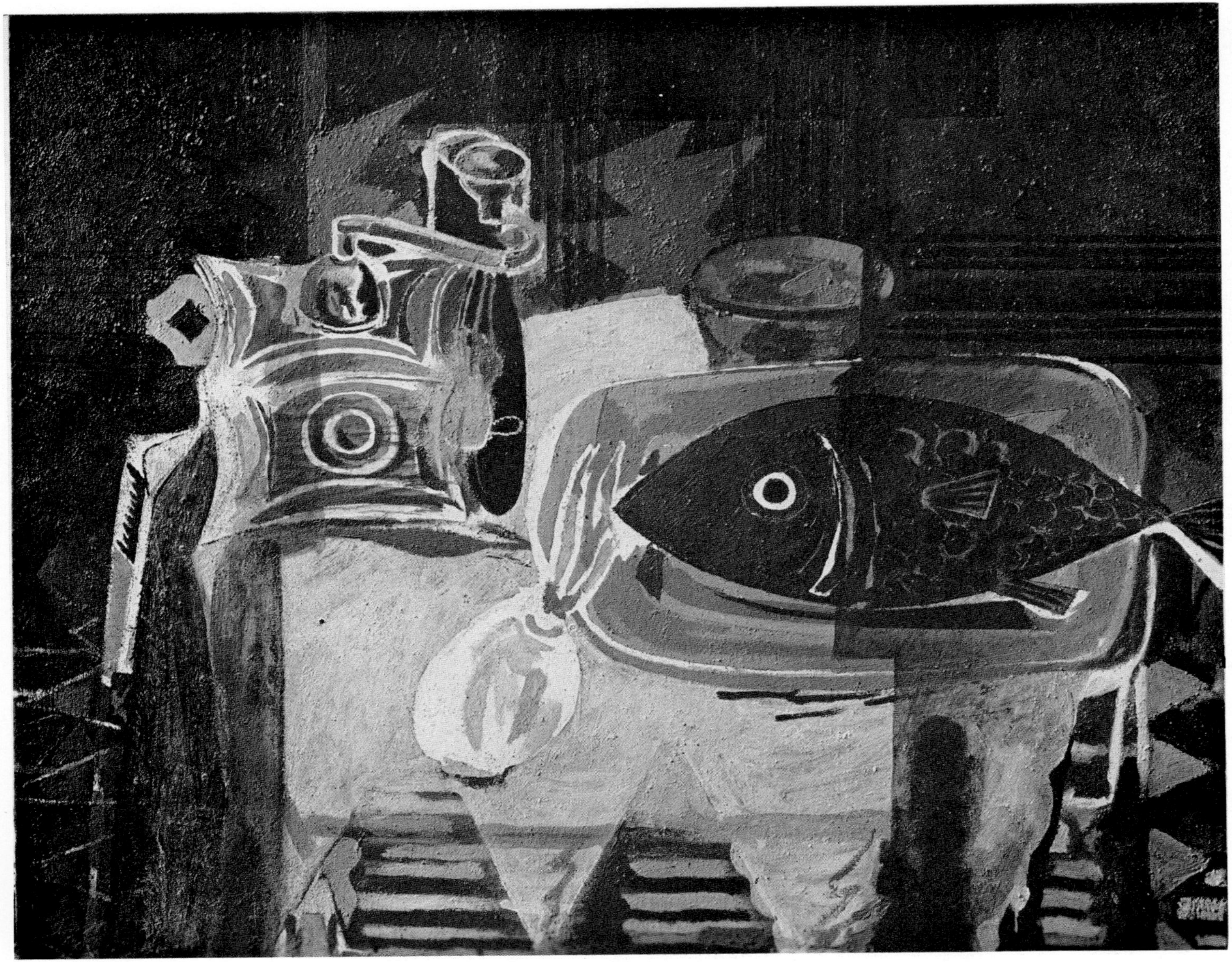

62 THE COFFEE MILL. 1942-43

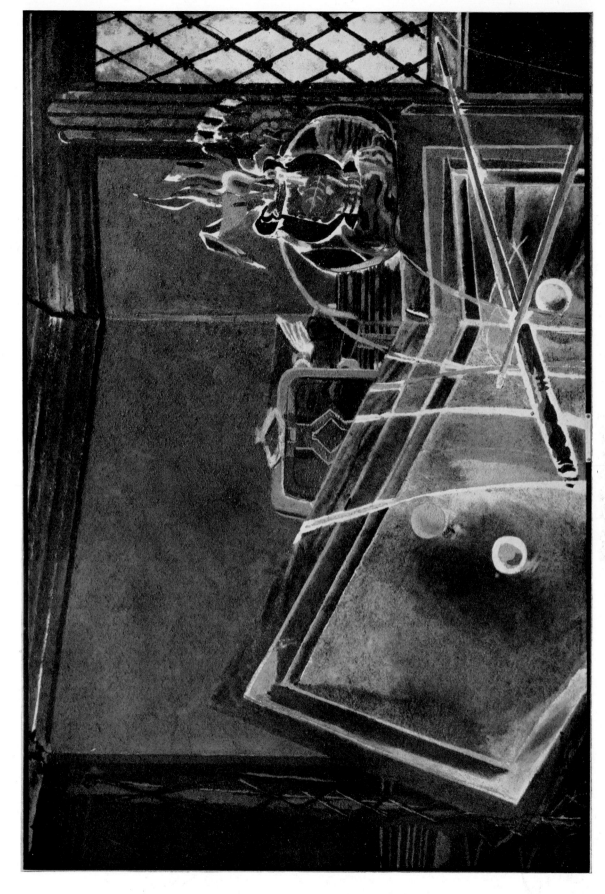

64 STILL LIFE. 1946

65 THE STUDIO, I. 1949

69 RECLINING WOMAN. 1930, completed in 1952

70 THE SHOWER. 1952

72 THE CHARIOT OF THE SUN. 1953-54

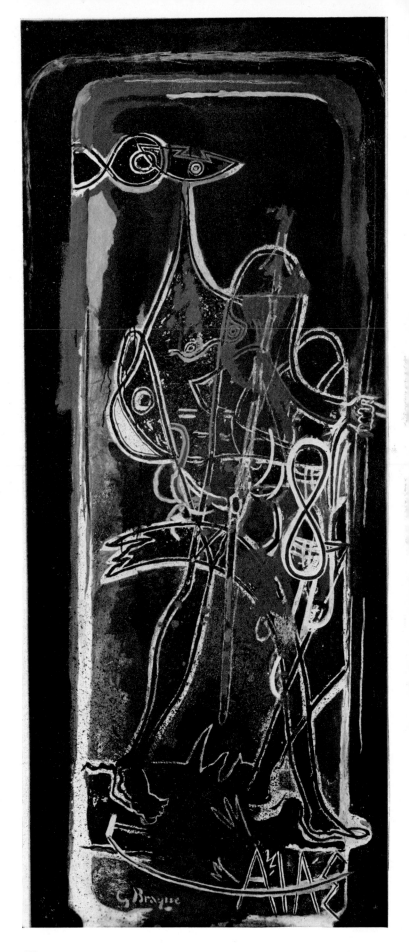

73 AJAX. 1955

74 LANDSCAPE WITH PLOUGH. 1955

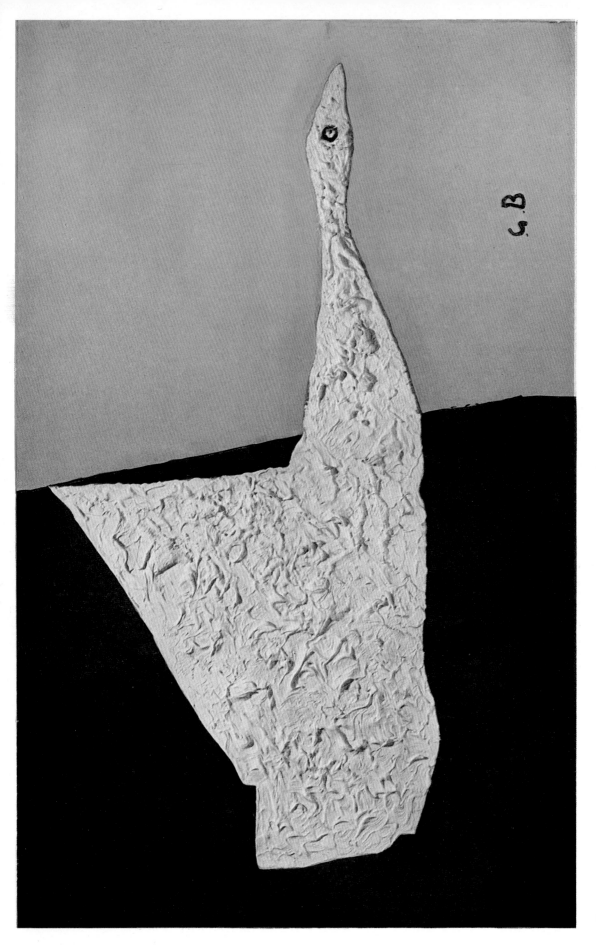

76 THE DUCK. 1956

77 THE BIRDS. 1957

78 THE BLACK BIRDS. 1957

79 NIGHT FLIGHT. 1959

80 THE BIRD AND ITS NEST. 1958

NOTES ON THE PLATES

BIBLIOGRAPHICAL NOTE

Most of the work on Braque that is of consequence has been written in English. I owe much to Henry R. Hope's *Braque* (Museum of Modern Art, New York, 1949), to the catalogue, by Douglas Cooper, of the Arts Council's Braque exhibition of 1956, and to three contributions by John Richardson: his essay on the *Atelier* series in the *Burlington Magazine* for June, 1955, his interview with Braque, published in *The Observer* on December 1st, 1957, and his *Braque* in the Penguin Modern Painters series (1958).

I have also drawn upon Braque's own reflections (*Le Jour et la Nuit*, Paris, 1952) and his statements to Dora Vallier in *Cahiers d'Art*, 1954, no. 1.

The quotations from Juan Gris are taken from the edition of his Letters collected by D. H. Kahnweiler, translated and edited by Douglas Cooper, and distributed by the St. George's Gallery (Books), 1956.

The quotation from the Goncourts' *French XVIII Century Painters* is from the abridged translation made by Robin Ironside and published by the Phaidon Press in 1948.

J. R.

NOTES ON THE PLATES

This list contains the original titles and comments by René Ben Sussan
on some of the paintings.

1. *Le mât, Anvers.* 1906. Private collection. 46 ×
33 cm.
Braque destroyed most of the work he had done
before his *fauve* paintings which he regards as his
first creative work. He was the youngest of the
fauve group, of which the most prominent artists
were Matisse and Marquet, who lived in the same
house on Quai St. Michel, Derain and Vlaminck,
the two boldest, who shared a studio at Le Chatou
near Paris, and Othon Friesz and Dufy, both born
at Le Havre, where they had met Braque and became friends. The adjective 'fauve' is due to the art
critic Louis Vauxcelles, who exclaimed in a room of
the Salon des Indépendants of 1905, where a conventional sculpture by Marque was surrounded by
paintings in bright colours: 'Donatello parmi les
fauves!'

2. *Le port d'Anvers.* 1906. Ottawa, National Gallery
of Canada. 50 × 61 cm.
In 1906 Braque and his friend Friesz spent the summer at Antwerp. The harbour inspired Braque to
paint many pictures, among them the well-known
Port d'Anvers in the collection of Baron van der
Heydt, Ascona, and a similar composition, *Le
bateau pavoisé à Anvers*, in the Kunstmuseum, Basle.

3. *Paysage d'Anvers.* 1906. Paris, private collection.
42 × 50 cm.
The brushwork, the harmony between violet pinks
and yellowish greens, is the same as in *Notre-Dame*,
1902, by Matisse. It shows that at this time Braque
was nearer to Matisse, a *fauve réfléchi*, than to the
more daring and impetuous Derain and Vlaminck,
who painted with practically pure colours.

4. *Paysage de l'Estaque.* 1906. Basle, Galerie Beyeler.
38 × 46 cm.
In the autumn of 1906 Braque went alone to
l'Estaque near Marseilles. The *fauves* had many
techniques and *manières*, the word *fauve* referring
merely to their great freedom of expression and
very bright colour. In the same year in which
Braque painted this picture, which—like the same

subject in the Musée de l'Annonciade at St.
Tropez—shows a greater care for composition, he
also painted in a looser *manière* with large dots,
leaving the canvas bare in places: *L'Estaque,
l'embarcadère* in the Musée National d'Art Moderne,
Paris, and in the following year *Petite baie à La
Ciotat*, formerly in the collection of Mme Bourdon,
Paris. The technique, derived from Neo-Impressionism, had been used earlier by Derain and twice
by Matisse, the second time being when he spent
the summer of 1904 with Signac and Cross at St.
Tropez.

5. *Le port de La Ciotat.* 1907. London, Mr. John Hay
Whitney. 65 × 81 cm.

6. *Maisons à l'Estaque.* 1908. Berne, Mr. and Mrs.
Hermann Rupf. 73 × 59,5 cm.
In November 1908, Braque exhibited at the Galerie
Kahnweiler the pictures which he had painted at
l'Estaque and which had been rejected by the jury
of the Salon d'Automne. The preface to the catalogue was by Guillaume Apollinaire.
Referring to *Maisons à l'Estaque* and to a much
smaller painting with only one house (formerly in
the collection of Dutilleul), Vauxcelles wrote in his
account of the exhibition in Gil Blas: 'Braque
méprise la forme, reduit tout, sites, figures et
maisons à des schémas géometriques, à des cubes.'
In the following spring he was to write about
Braque's *bizarreries cubiques*. For the second time the
art critic who had decried Cézanne gave a name to
an art movement: *cubisme*. The change is not only
from fauvism to Cézanneism in the landscapes of
l'Estaque dated 1906 and 1908; it is of deeper significance. Anecdote (the people walking, Plate 4) has
disappeared, the houses have neither doors nor
windows, as in *La maison derrière les arbres* (Mr.
Lehman, New York). The conception of the per-
ceptible spectacle is radically changed from objective to subjective. This was the beginning of a
revolution which Braque and Picasso were to carry
much further in the following years.

7. *Paysage de l'Estaque*. 1908. Paris, Musée National d'Art Moderne. 46 × 38 cm.

Fauvism had not been a revolution, but an impetuous exaltation of Neo-Impressionism. 'On ne saurait toujours rester dans le paroxysme', Braque said later in explaining why the end of 1907 saw the end of his *fauve* period, during which he had painted less than thirty pictures. The Cézanne retrospective exhibition held in the Salon d'Automne of 1907 very strongly impressed Braque and his fauve friends. Cézanne made them aware that their *paroxysme* could lead them no further. The fireworks are put out; in self-punishment, fulgurant reds and yellows are burnt down to ochres, bright blues to ashy greys. Viridian green, however, was still permissible.

8. *Le port*. 1908. Warrenton, Virginia, Mr. Walter P. Chrysler, Jr. 81 × 81 cm.

At the end of 1907 Braque had painted the *Vue de l'Hôtel Mistral, l'Estaque* (Mr. Werner E. Josten, New York) from memory, and he now painted this harbour scene from imagination, in order to 'free himself from models'. Through imagination he achieves a composition in which the rhythm is not that of an objectively given scenery, but that necessitated by subjective feeling and by the four sides of a two-dimensional canvas, and in which there is no receding background, no going through. Sky and sea are painted as solidly as the rest, a first attempt at 'tactile' feeling. The rhythm urges him to prolong the curve of the clewed-up sail at the right of a cloud, the left of which are two parallels to the spars. The horizontal line of the sea is extended into the breakwater on the right. These prolongations of shapes into one another were to occur in most of his later paintings. Compare for instance the drawer intersecting the playing card in Plate 16, the upper horizontal edge of the table extended through the guitar in Plate 26, and in a later seascape, Plate 68, the curves of the sandbanks intermixed with the curves of the boat hulls, and the culminating interlocking of shapes in the *Studios*, Plates 66-67.

9. *La Roche-Guyon: Le château*. 1909. Stockholm, Mr. Rolf de Maré. 81 × 60 cm.

Another version is in a private collection at Roubaix.

10. *Piano et guitare*. 1909-10. New York, Solomon R. Guggenheim Museum. 92 × 43 cm.

Braque now returned to l'Estaque, but instead of landscapes he now painted still-lifes in ascending rhythms—emphasised here by the vertical keyboard of the piano. The modelling in small facets with sharp edges is given by different directions of light, as in some pictures by El Greco, of which one is here reminded by the movement of the sinuous ascending rhythm and by the concertina shape on the left of the candle. The picture has a pendant, *Violon et palette*, in the same collection.

11. *Violon et cruche*. 1910. Basle, Kunstmuseum. 117 × 73,5 cm.

At the top, behind the pitcher, a sheet of paper is placed to fill the space and to avoid, by hiding it, a receding background—a means of bringing the complete representation to the surface of the canvas, creating thus a space which Braque defines as *espace tactile*. He used this device in many later pictures—planes which are thus placed with the same aim, but which are no longer representations of paper or any other object and which seem arbitrary. See Plates 27, 43, 44.

12. *Buste de jeune fille*. About 1910. Washington, Mr. and Mrs. Bralove collection. 65 × 54 cm.

This picture, which is now also entitled *Femme à la croix*, was among the last which Braque painted during the first cubist phase, a phase when the idiom of Cézanne, carried a step further, abolished perspective, post-Renaissance illusionism and, above all, the aerial perspective and fleeting visions of Impressionism.

13. *Le portugais*. 1911. Basle, Kunstmuseum, 117 × 81,5 cm.

At this period of their friendship, the aesthetic views of Braque and Picasso were identical. To them, the shaping of objects in crystal form still meant a three-dimensional representation of forms and space. They were concerned with the fundamental problem of painting: the representation of coloured volumes on the flat surface of the canvas, which they regard as the only space of their conception: *l'espace pictural*. Facing such a momentous problem, they decided to leave out colour for the time being and to face in neutral tones the problem of form. They dissected the form of objects and showed them not only as seen from different angles, but also from the inside and from the knowledge they had of the objects. Juan Gris, who joined the two friends in their researches, called this phase *cubisme analytique*. See Plates 14, 15.

Le portugais is a conceptual representation of a man holding a guitar, by means of lines and modulated tones. Letters and numbers, which have no thickness, are here introduced for the first time as two-dimensional plastic elements, and painted with stencils as used on packing cases.

14. *Le guéridon*. 1911-12. Paris, Musée National d'Art Moderne. 116×81 cm.

15. *Nature morte au violon*. 1912. Paris, private collection. 116×81 cm.

In *Les Peintres cubistes* (1913), Guillaume Apollinaire wrote about the colour of Braque's paintings: 'la nacre de ses tableaux irise notre entendement.' And about form: 'Braque a enseigné aux hommes et aux autres peintres l'usage esthétique de formes si inconnues que quelques poètes seuls les avaient soupçonnées.'

16. *Composition à l'as de trèfle*. 1912-13. Paris, Musée National d'Art Moderne. Oil and charcoal on canvas, 81×60 cm.

In paintings such as *Femme lisant* (M. Raoul La Roche, Paris) and *Homme au violon* (Mme. Ch. Bührle, Zurich), both of 1911, the gap separating them from nature was so considerable that their degree of legibility was regarded as *hermétique*. Braque, like Picasso, had reached the limit of the experience of *cubisme analytique*, in which colour was excluded. Both felt the need to revise, not their theories—they had none—but their conceptions. The new conceptions led them to the third phase of cubism, which Juan Gris, in his dogmatic spirit, called *cubisme synthétique*. Colour is introduced, not as part of a coloured object, but simultaneously to the conceptual shapes of the objects. Braque experiments with colour by introducing in his composition cut-out shapes of coloured paper related to the drawing, which intersects them in brush work or charcoal pencil. Using this, the *papier collé* (cf. Plates 18, 19, 26), he made a study for the *Composition à l'as de trèfle*. The paper he used was a wallpaper which imitated wood panelling. In the oil painting (Plate 16), the wood is imitated by a comb as used by house painters. Braque had been an apprentice house painter in his father's shop in Le Havre and also in Paris in 1900, and knew all the devices that were in use to imitate all kinds of wood

grain, sham marble, stone, etc. Compare the imitations of wood in Plates 17, 43, 51, 55, 64.

17. *Femme à la guitare*. 1913. Paris, Musée National d'Art Moderne. 130,3×73,7 cm.

In the following year, 1914, Braque painted *L'homme à la guitare* (M. André Lefèvre, Paris), which is in the same spirit and the same size and may be regarded as a pendant to the above.

18. *Guitare et programme de cinéma*. 1913. Paris, M. Pablo Picasso. Pasted paper, 60×73 cm.

The use of *papier collé* was not only a means of experiencing colour in compositions which had hitherto been multitudinous monochrome ideograms, it was also used by Braque to introduce a feeling of reality—not realism—from which he had completely digressed. Here he uses a programme of a cinema in Sorgues and a piece of wallpaper imitating wood panelling. The manner of using larger planes led him also to a simplification which allowed further developments. Cf. Plates 20 and 26.

19. *La table du musicien*. 1913. Basle, Kunstmuseum. 65×92 cm.

This picture, which is completely painted in oils, evolves from the *papiers collés*.

20. *Verre et violon*. 1913-14. Basle, Kunstmuseum. Oil, charcoal and pasted paper on canvas, 116× 80,5 cm.

21. *Musique*. 1914. Washington, Phillips Gallery. 91,5×59,7 cm.

In an earlier picture, *Nature morte à la grappe de raisins* of 1912 (D.-H. Kahnweiler, Paris), Braque had already mixed sand into the paint. The aim was to get a more concrete tactile feeling of the painted surface and also to ensure that the reflection of light should not affect the intensity of tone. Preoccupied with textures, he here also mixed in sawdust—a device he had learned from house-painting. At a soirée given by the art-dealer Paul Guillaume in the winter 1917-18, Guillaume Apollinaire gave a lecture on 'La naissance de l'Art tactile'.

22. *La bouteille de rhum*. 1914. Private collection. 46×55 cm.

Here, as in *Musique*, the dots are used to create textures on the various flat grounds. This was not, as has been written, under the influence of Seurat. They are also an imitation of a cheap wall-paper of that time, patterned with dark and light dots on a ground of medium strength. Cf. Plates 23, 24, 27, 29.

23. *Verre, fruits et carte à jouer.* 1917. Paris, private collection. 38 × 55 cm.
Braque resumes the work interrupted by the war. This still-life is painted like his *Bouteille de rhum* (Plate 22) of three years earlier, the new feature being a composition inscribed in an almond shape, which he uses in many other paintings of 1917-18, along with more geometric shapes: lozenges as in the two still-lifes in the Kröller-Müller Museum, Otterlo, octagons divided into spiderweb-like areas as in *Le Gobelet*, A. E. Gallatin Collection, Philadelphia Museum of Art.

24. *La Musicienne.* 1917-18. Basle, Kunstmuseum. 220,5 × 112,5 cm.
Compared to the same subject in *Femme à la guitare* (Plate 17), *La Musicienne* shows a further step towards monumental rhythm and for the first time the complete achievement of Braque's aim: *l'espace pictural*, which to him is the reverse of the traditional space, in which the eye is led from the surface to the receding backgrounds; here contrariwise the picture protrudes towards the spectator. In spite of the very large size of the picture one is reminded of medieval miniatures by the flat laid colours, green, red, and blue, of the vertical planes, by the pattern on the floor and by the carriage of the figure. *La Musicienne*, like most of Braque's work, is painted so fervently that it gives a religious feeling. It has been jokingly said that for cubist painters the theme of *Femme à la guitare* had replaced that of *Madonna and Child*.

25. *Le guéridon.* 1918. Eindhoven, Stedelijk van Abbe Museum, 130 × 74 cm.
In reaction to the rigidity of the geometric still-lifes and of *La musicienne*, Braque painted the *Nature morte sur un guéridon* (Philadelphia Museum of Art, Arensberg Collection), in which the rigid edges of the planes are replaced by a profusion of undulating curves. Here, in *Le guéridon*, the reaction is more to the flat-laid paint, by loose brush work, on black priming, creating lively transparent textures. From 1911 to 1942, still-lifes on guéridons were for Braque a favourite theme. Cf. Plates 14, 15, 16, 29, 44, 45, 59.

26. *Guitare et clarinette.* 1918. Philadelphia Museum of Art, Louise and Walter Arensberg collection. Pasted paper, corrugated cardboard, gouache and charcoal on cardboard. 77,2 × 95 cm.
A *papier collé* outstanding in the perfect balance of shapes of beautiful amplitude. Drawing is reduced to a minimum. The papers used are of various textures, including corrugated paper, also used in 1917-18 by the sculptor Henri Laurens, who had been attracted to the cubist group in 1913 by their *papiers collés*, and was Braque's disciple. The use of a relief paper was very likely inspired by the sculptor, whose work also induced the painter, at this period, to paint several still-lifes on plaster.

27. *Le buffet.* 1919. Paris, private collection. 80 × 100 cm.
Braque was now in full possession of his means. The use of dark and light, warm and cold planes creates light, a light which does not issue from any source. Light and shadows are considered as tangible shapes as in the black shadow underlining the musical score, or as in the two shades of the glass.

28. *Nature morte sur une cheminée.* 1919. Paris, ex Léonce Rosemberg collection. Gouache on wood, 26 × 14 cm.
The very small size of this painting underlines the magnitude of Braque's composition; it is as monumental as in his largest canvases. Cf. the same theme on Plate 33.

29. *Café Bar.* 1919. Basle, Kunstmuseum. 160 × 82 cm.
A masterly *guéridon* supporting a piled-up still-life in the interior of a café-bar. Imitations of wood grain and wallpaper are used, with lettering in Napoleon III style such as was used on shop fronts by house painters. Lettering in the same style, reduced to 'fé-bar' is used in the same subject of the Philadelphia Museum of Art. Braque exceptionally gives to this picture a receding depth, not by perspective, but by his conception of light (cf. note on Plate 27), here a chiaroscuro given by the indented white shape at the bottom right, the light on the foot and the left side of the table, the white fruit dish, pipe, musical score and the lettering. The black tiling, which is not in perspective, is cleverly prolonged at the top by indented black shapes, a

counterpoint to the indented white shapes at the bottom.

30. *Nature morte à la sonate.* About 1920. Paris, Musée de la Ville. 35,5 × 65 cm.

31. *Compotier et clarinette.* 1920. Berne, Mr. and Mrs. Hermann Rupf. 34,5 × 65 cm.
The rigidity of shapes is by degrees replaced by a sensual looseness which gives a riper fullness to the forms. With objects as simple as a bunch of grapes in a fruit dish, two pears, one cut, a glass, a clarinet and a sheet of paper on a marble table, Braque creates a painted poem. 'Le peintre pense en formes et en couleurs, l'objet c'est la poétique,' he says.

32. *Canéphores.* 1922. Paris, private collection. Each 180 × 72,2 cm.
Without deviating from his two-dimensional conception of the *espace pictural*, in these two large painted caryatids Braque contrives a sculptural relief by means of drawing only; there is no modeling in the ample loose forms. The tan colour of the figures and the creamy ornate shapes of what we have to call lights pervade in what we have perforce to call the background, accentuating the impression of looseness and illustrating Braque's statement: 'La forme et la couleur ne se confondent pas. Il y a simultanéité.' Because the sensuality of these figures has been conceived with a discreetness characteristic of Braque, it has been wrongly said they were painted as still-lifes, and with the same detachment; there is no detachment in Braque's work—fervour would be the right word. Renoir and the 'classic' period of Picasso have been, with no reason, quoted with regard to these two decorative panels which, in fact, are rooted in the French tradition, that of Louis XIV decorative tapestries, with which they are closely akin in the orchestration of their ample forms. Cf. Plate 37.

33. *La cheminée.* 1922. St. Louis (Missouri), Mr. and Mrs. Richard K. Weil. 130 × 74 cm.
As early as 1911, Braque had painted still-lifes on mantelshelves, in which the decoration under the shelf balanced the shapes of the objects on top. Later he painted mantelpieces (cf. Plate 28) allowing vertical compositions as in his *guéridons*. There are many versions of *Cheminées*, which, like the *Guéridons*, were a favourite theme until 1927, when he painted a replica of the earlier picture of 1923 in

the Kunsthaus, Zurich. In the *Cheminées* the 'faux marbre' of house painters replaces the wood grain imitation of the *Guéridons*. The richest imitation of marble is in the version of 1925 owned by Mr. and Mrs. Samuel A. Marx, Chicago, and in *La table de marbre*, Plate 36.

34. *Fruits, pichet et pipe.* 1924. Private Collection, U.S.A. 42 × 64 cm.

35. *Verre et coupe de porcelaine.* 1924. Zurich, Mrs. Ch. Bührle-Schalk. 31 × 65,5 cm.

36. *La table de marbre.* 1925. Paris, Musée National d'Art Moderne. 131 × 73,5 cm.
By its composition, with a still-life crowding half the upper part of the picture, *La table de marbre* is closely related to the *Guéridons* and to the *Cheminées* (cf. note on Plate 33).

37. *Canéphore.* 1926. Washington, National Gallery of Art, Chester Dale Collection. 161,3 × 74 cm.
Like the *Canéphores* of 1922, this painting is reminiscent of *Le Grand Siècle*. We can imagine this monumental basket-bearer translated into stone in the gardens of Versailles. From 1922 to 1926 Braque painted a series of half-length semi-nudes of which *Canéphore*, 1925, in the same collection, and *Femme nue assise*, 1925, in the Fukushima collection, Tokyo, are the most beautiful versions. At the same period Braque made a series of related drawings in red chalk, pencil and charcoal. The basket-bearer induced him to introduce a new object in his still-lifes; many at this period consist of flowers or fruits in baskets.

38. *La rose noire.* 1927. Meriden, Conn., Mrs. Burton Tremaine. 50,7 × 92 cm.
At first sight this very rich still-life seems to be lit from the left, but then the inner side of the fruit dish would be dark on the left and light on the right, which it is not, likewise the rose would not be as in counter light. Braque, by planes of light (the white vertical rectangle on the left for instance) and dark planes, expresses light in plastic tangible shapes (cf. note on Plate 27). To differentiate the textures of the white painted parts of the patterned table cloth and of the fruit dish, Braque, with a blunt point running in all directions of the still wet thick-laid paint, imitates the craquelures of earthenware.

39. *La table.* 1928. Washington, National Gallery of Art, Chester Dale Collection. 81,3 × 130,8 cm.

40. *Citrons et serviette.* 1928. Washington, Phillips Gallery. 41 × 121 cm.

41. *Barques sur la plage, Dieppe.* 1929. Neviges, Collection Mr. and Mrs. W. Schniewind. 50 × 65 cm.
Braque had not been tempted by landscape painting since his stay at La Roche-Guyon twenty years earlier. Returning to Normandy he paints seascapes. In his still-lifes, it is possible to follow his successive steps; the long gap of time in which there are no landscapes to compare with the early seascapes of Antwerp, l'Estaque and La Ciotat, enables us to measure at once the considerable enrichment of Braque's *langage pictural*. A cottage was built for him at Varengeville, near Dieppe, in 1931, where he was to spend every summer and paint seascapes, either from memory or from small pencil sketches, in which boats, tar-black or coloured, rest on the spotted pattern of the pebbles. (Cf. Plates 1, 2, 3, 5, 8, 68, 71.)

42. *Nature morte.* 1929. Private collection, Switzerland. 97 × 130 cm.
The traditional cubist fruit dish is here replaced by a basket. (Cf. note on Plate 37.) A similar basket is found in *La nappe jaune*, 1935, owned by Mr. and Mrs. Samuel A. Marx, Chicago, a picture which was awarded the first prize at the International Exhibition at the Carnegie Institute in 1937.

43. *Le Jour.* 1929. Washington, National Gallery of Art, Chester Dale Collection. 115 × 147 cm.

44. *La table ronde.* 1929. Washington, Phillips Gallery. 147 × 114 cm.

45. *La bouteille de marc.* 1930. New York, private collection. 130,2 × 74 cm.

46. *Zélos, Niké.* 1931. Paris, Collection M. Aimé Maeght. Plaster, incised, 186 × 95 cm.

47. *Heraclès.* 1931. Paris, Collection M. Aimé Maeght. Plaster, incised, 186 × 105 cm.
On large plaster slabs coated with black paint, Braque incised mythological divinities in white

linear curves in aerial rhythms such as are appropriate to deities. They are inspired by engraved Greek and Etruscan bronze mirrors.
These plaster panels, four in number, made for the decoration of an apartment, are related to the sixteen engravings on copper commissioned in 1930 by the art dealer Ambroise Vollard for the illustration of Hesiod's Theogony. The book, like many commissions of Vollard, was not published. In 1955, however, it was finally brought out by M. Aimé Maeght. Other incised plaster slabs followed. In some of them, large portions of the coating are taken out and left either white or painted in colour, opposing balanced planes to the linear rhythms. (Cf. Plates 72, 73.)

48. *La plage.* 1931. Warrenton, Virginia, Mr. Walter P. Chrysler Jr. 130 × 195 cm.
A parallel has been drawn between Braque's *Baigneuses* and those Picasso painted in 1928 at Dinard; but there is no other parallel than that of the two confronting walls, one assigned to each of the two friends, in the Galerie Paul Rosemberg, rue La Boétie, on which their pictures could be seen from 1924 to 1939. Picasso's *Baigneuses* which are, by a combination of shapes and bright colour stripes, bathing cabins as much as bathers, are engaged in tremendously dynamic ball-play, and differ totally, both in spirit and pictorially, from those of Braque. In *La plage* the style has changed into a linear one, no doubt because of Braque's work on the incised plaster slabs and the engravings for Hesiod's Theogony. Also, whereas the paint had been laid on thick, it is, in this period, laid on in a thin film. There are many versions of *Baigneuses* in small and large format. (Cf. Plate 69.)

49. *Nature morte.* 1933. Paris, M. Georges Braque. 97 × 130 cm.
A white graphism, as in the incised plaster slabs (Plates 46, 47), is here achieved by scratching with a sharp point the thin layer of paint, leaving the canvas bare (Cf. Plate 50.)
In Jean Paulhan's *Braque le patron* the painter exclaims: 'Ah, je ne sais pas si ce que j'entame ici sera falaise ou femme'; it explains the cucurbitaceous shape which we see in this still-life and that on Plate 50, as well as on the reclining bather, Plate 48, and which is also found on the top of cliffs of some of his seascapes.

50. *Nature morte.* 1934. Basle, Kunstmuseum. Emanuel Hoffmann Stiftung. 54×65 cm.

51. *Nature morte à la mandoline.* 1935. New York, Mrs. Louis Bergman. 130,2×162 cm.
By the paint laid on thick again, the wood grain imitation, the use of wall paper patterns, Braque seems to retrace his steps to 1928-29. There is, however, in this still-life an important difference in the style. Compared to the serene equilibrium of *Le Jour* (Plate 43), the style is here one of great animation, emphasised by the zigzag pattern in the mandolin and the wallpaper. It is amusing to see the old-fashioned wallpaper replaced here by a 'modern' one, inspired by Braque's own revolution, which had completely transformed even the minor *arts décoratifs*. But the important new feature of this picture is in the three curved black lines which prolong at the top of the wallpaper the shape of the table and create an extension of space, a depth expressed not by aerial perspective, but by flat plastic means. These three curves are the forerunners of the vertical and slightly slanted lines used for the same purpose in the *Studios*, cf. Plate 66.

52. *Femme peignant.* 1936. Chicago, Mr. Nathan Cummings. 92×73 cm.
Except for the few portraits painted before his fauve 'first creative work', Braque painted no portraits: 'Un portrait! Et d'une fille en bijoux encore. Non, je n'ai pas l'esprit assez dominateur'. (In *Braque le patron* by Jean Paulhan).

53. *Femme au chapeau.* 1937. Paris, Mme. Jacqueline Delubac. 92×92 cm.
The conception of a figure seen in profile and from the front has its source in *cubisme analytique*, when Braque and Picasso were concerned in analysing shapes seen from different angles. Cf. the very similar version, Plate 52, and the head of the reclining figure in Plate 48. Braque, like Picasso and Matisse, felt the need to express a subject in exhaustive versions. A third version, *La femme peintre*, in oblong format, is in the collection of Mr. and Mrs. Samuel A. Marx, Chicago.

54. *Nature morte aux raisins et aux fleurs.* 1934-39. Private collection, U.S.A. 65×80 cm.

55. *L'atelier.* 1939. Private collection, U.S.A. 114,3×146 cm.

This first *Studio* initiates a series of still-lifes in interior scenes, the *Ateliers* of ten years later, numbered I to IX (cf. Plates 65, 66, 67). We see also the first appearance of the theme of the bird (Plates 66, 67, 76, 77, 78, 79, 80) on the canvas on the easel, the canvas showing for the first time an X broken shape as in the table, Plate 61, and as in the series of *Billards*, Plate 63.

56. *Intérieur à la palette.* 1941. Private Collection, Italy. 100×100 cm.

57. *La table de cuisine au gril.* 1942. Zurich, Collection Mr. Gustav Zumsteg. 130×73,5 cm.
A still-life in the tradition of the *Guéridons*, but in an interior scene and a new style; the setting and the object-performers have changed. In 1942-43 Braque painted a series of still-lifes with fishes: *Les poissons noirs* and *La carafe* in smaller oblong format in the Musée National d'Art Moderne Paris (cf. also Plates 60 and 62). A simpler version of the above, *La table de cuisine*, is owned by M. Jean Paulhan.

58. *Grappe de raisin et pot sur une commode.* 1941. Mme. Lily Pons, U.S.A.

59. *Le guéridon rose.* 1942. Paris, Collection S.B. 104×45 cm.

60. *Nature morte au poisson et à la carafe.* 1943. Stockholm, private collection.

61. *Le tapis vert.* 1943. Paris, Musée National d'Art Moderne. 38×55 cm.
As in Plate 60, the very thick tactile impasto on the wall brings it forward, at hand reach, at the same front level of the still-life painted thin in contrast, a new device used by Braque in his conception of the *espace pictural*: 'Quand une nature morte n'est pas à la portée de la main, elle cesse d'être une nature morte.'

62. *Le moulin à café.* 1942-43. Private Collection, U.S.A. 87×105 cm.

63. *Le billard.* 1945. Paris, Musée National d'Art Moderne. 130×194 cm.
'Le conformisme commence à la définition,' 'Il ne faut pas imiter ce que l'on veut créer,' 'Le peintre ne tache pas de reconstituer une anecdote, mais de

constituer un fait pictural.' These statements by Braque help us to comprehend his art, and this picture, better than all the unsatisfactory 'explanations' which have been given for the tilting of the table. There are several versions of the 'Billard' theme. Two other important versions are in the collections of Mr. Leigh Block, Chicago, and Mr. Gelman, Mexico.

64. *Nature morte.* 1946. U.S.A., Private Collection. 81×60 cm.

65. *Atelier I.* 1949. Paris, Private Collection. 92× 73 cm.
Though this Studio is numbered I, its conception is so far from that of the eight others which Braque painted from 1949 to 1956 that it should be considered apart in the series of this theme, which is so important in the work of the artist. Cf. the *Studio* painted ten years earlier, Plate 55, and Plates 66 and 67.

66. *Atelier III.* 1949. Basle, Hänngi Collection. 144×175 cm. (Formerly called *Atelier V.*)
'Impregnation, obsession, hallucination' are the steps which lead Braque to creation. Impregnated by his conceptions of space, rhythm, shapes and colours, impregnated and obsessed by a theme, the hallucination produces this series of *Ateliers*, which are not a representation of his own studio, but the poetic vision of a studio expressed in painting. 'Il faut se contenter de découvrir, mais se guarder d'expliquer. Chaque preuve diminue la vérité.' This statement, valid for the artist, is also conclusive for the critic; to analyse, to 'explain' these pictures is useless: 'il n'est en art qu'une chose qui vaille: celle que l'on ne peut expliquer.'

67. *Atelier VI.* 1950. Paris, Collection M. Aimé Maeght. 130×162,5 cm.
With the exception of *Atelier VIII*, owned by Mr. Douglas Cooper, which is in relatively bright colours, the eight other *Studios* are painted in black and grey harmony enlivened with pale colours.

68. *Marine.* 1950. Geneva, Private Collection. 46×61 cm. Cf. note on Plate 41.

69. *Femme couchée.* 1930-52. Paris, Collection M. Aimé Maeght. 73 × 180 cm.

In his studio Braque is surrounded by many canvases in various states of completion, on which he works according to his mood. This large reclining figure, started with the series of *Baigneuses* (cf. Plate 48) in 1930, has been finished twenty-two years later. The picture, an almost monochrome dark-grey harmony, modulated like the cubist paintings of 1912, is like an epitome of forty years of Braque's work. *Nu couché*, owned by the artist, started in 1932 and finished in 1951, is painted in large flat surfaces of yellow, white, light grey and light tan. The contrast of the conception of these two pictures of the same theme shows that Braque's obsession is never uncontrolled: 'Tout état est toujours complémentaire de l'état qui l'a précédé.'

70. *La pluie.* 1952. Washington, Phillips Gallery. 35,5×55 cm.
With his *Vanitas* of 1939, the *Tournesols* of 1943 (formerly in the collection of Mme. Jacqueline Delubac) and the *Sunflowers* of 1946 (collection of *Reader's Digest*, New York), Braque had already made a step towards 'un retour à la nature' which seems to contradict his conceptions; but he says: 'Ne jamais adhérer' and shows his freedom of mind and contempt for theories. He painted such 'naturalistic' landscapes from 1952 to 1957. Cf. Plates 74 and 77.

71. *Marine.* 1953. Paris, private collection. 17× 28 cm.
A 'divertissement' of great charm painted on the wooden lid of a box of 'calissons' (sweets from Aix-en-Provence).

72. *Le char du Soleil.* 1953-54. Zurich, M. Gustav Zumsteg. Plaster painted in relief, 22×27 cm.
A reversed composition of the plaster relief *Io* of 1939. The *Femme debout* of 1920, *Hymen* of 1939 and *Hesperis* of 1939 are among the sculptures which Braque made before the Occupation, a period when, owing to the scarcity of oil paints and canvas, he was active as a sculptor and made the *Poisson* of 1943, the *Tête de cheval* of 1943 and many heads. His sculptures are characterised by their flatness: like medals, they should be looked at only from two sides, as they are made of two relief profiles.

73. *Ajax.* 1955. Chicago, Mr. and Mrs. Samuel A. Marx. 180×72 cm.

This impressive painting is related to the incised plaster slabs of 1931. Cf. Plates 46 and 47.

74. *Paysage à la charrue*. 1955. Paris, M. Aimé Maeght collection. 34 × 64 cm.
La plaine I and *La plaine II*, both of 1956, are versions without the plough. At the same period Braque painted a series of very narrow and very oblong landscapes, consisting of a strip of sky and a strip of field or sea, the horizon expressing a new conception of space cf. note on Plate 70.

75. *Nature morte*. 1955. Oslo, Mr. Ragnar Moltzau. 73 × 87 cm.
A larger version, painted in 1956, is in the collection of M. Aimé Maeght, Paris. In this picture, which is elsewhere almost identical, the fruit dish has been replaced by a bird and a newspaper.

76. *Le canard*. 1956. Paris, Private Collection. 60 × 84 cm.
See notes on Plates 78 and 79.

77. *Les oiseaux*. 1957. Private Collection. 24 × 41 cm. Cf. Plates 70 and 74.

78. *Les oiseaux noirs*. 1957. Paris, M. Aimé Maeght collection. 129 × 181 cm. in a frame painted by the artist.
Braque had been commissioned to paint three ceiling panels for the Etruscan Room in the Musée du Louvre, which he carried out in 1952-53. They consist of black birds delineated by a broad white halo and flying in deep blue Mediterranean sky. He had also painted birds in his series of *Ateliers* (cf. Plates 66, 67). From 1956 to this day he has been obsessed by the theme of Birds, which inspired a great number of drawings, lithographs, etchings, gouache and oil paintings. He had been impressed by the flights of birds in the flat and boundless country of Camargue in the South o France. To him the theme is a *fait pictural*, in which he expresses his new conception of space, and has no esoteric meaning as has been suggested. It is the privilege of a great master that the spectators may attribute to his work what meaning they choose. In the picture *A tire d'aile* of 1956, a brownish-black bird flies in a sky painted in such heavy impasto, increasing at the bottom, that through the light-blue ether the clods of earth can almost be felt.

79. *Vol de nuit*. 1959. Paris, M. Georges Braque. 80,5 × 155 cm.
Le canard (Plate 76) leaves the black night towards the light. Here the bird has left the daylight and flies through the night of a sky painted in a thick tactile impasto, but yet suggestive of interstellar space.

80. *L'oiseau et son nid*. 1958. Paris, M. Georges Braque 113 × 131 cm.
An earlier and simpler version, painted in 1956, is in Braque's country house at Varengeville.

ACKNOWLEDGEMENTS

Grateful acknowledgement is made to M. Georges Braque for his courteous help and ready advice during the preparation of this volume. The artist's secretary, Mlle Lachaud, gave valuable assistance. We are also grateful to M. Aimé Maeght as well as to Mme Mangin of Galerie Maeght for giving useful information and for placing photographs at our disposal.

Thanks are also due to all Museum authorities and private owners who have given permission for their pictures to be reproduced, in particular: Musée National d'Art Moderne, Paris; Musée de la Ville de Paris; Oeffentliche Kunstsammlung, Kunstmuseum, Basle; National Gallery of Canada, Ottawa; National Gallery of Art, Washington (Chester Dale Collection); Phillips Gallery, Washington; Mons. S. B., Paris; Galerie Beyeler, Basle; Mme Ch. Bührle-Schalk, Zurich; Mme Jacqueline Delubac, Paris; Mr. Rolf de Maré, Stockholm; Mr. Ragnar Moltzau, Oslo; Mr. and Mrs. Hermann Rupf, Berne; Mr. and Mrs. W. Schniewind, Neviges; Mrs. Burton Tremaine, Meriden, Conn.; H.E. the United States Ambassador in London, the Hon. John H. Whitney; Mr. Gustav Zumsteg, Zurich.

SOURCES OF PHOTOGRAPHS

Museum photographs: 2, 11, 13, 19, 20, 21, 24, 29, 37, 39, 40, 43, 44, 50; Archives Photographiques, Paris: 16, 25, 26, 28, 30, 34, 63; Walter Dräyer, Zurich: 33, 57, 72, 75; Giraudon, Paris: 10, 14, 52; Hans Hinz, Basle: 35; Lanièpce, Paris: 3, 7, 15, 17, 23, 27, 36, 49, 53, 59, 61, 65, 67, 76, 79; Jakob Lauri, Berne: 31; Galerie Louise Leiris: 1, 8, 9, 12, 18, 22; Routhier, Paris (by courtesy of Galerie Maeght): 32, 46, 47, 48, 51, 54, 56, 58, 60, 62, 64, 66, 68, 69, 70, 71, 73, 74, 77; H. Schmölz, Cologne: 41; Marc Vaux, Paris: 42; Vizzavona, Paris: 4; Z. Wegner, London: 5.